We Got to Play Baseball

60 Stories from Men
Who Played the Game

Gregg Olson
and
Ocean Palmer

Strategic Book Publishing and Rights Co.

Strategic Book Publishing and Rights Co.
12620 FM 1960, Suite A4-507
Houston, TX 77065

FIRST EDITION

Book jacket photograph courtesy of the Baltimore Orioles and Major League Baseball

Library of Congress Cataloging-in-Publication Data

Simendinger, Theodore J. and Olson, Greggory William

We Got to Play Baseball/Theodore J. Simendinger as "Ocean Palmer" and Greggory William (Gregg) Olson. 1st edition. Originally registered as Sideshow.

ISBN: 978-1-61897-285-9

1. Non-fiction   2. Sports   3. Baseball   4. By Title

Library of Congress Control Number: TXu001707155

10 9 8 7 6 5 4 3 2 1

Design: Dedicated Book Services, Inc.

Dedications

A baseball life is a great life but not an easy one. Behind every player is a loving and supporting family that trades thousands of hours at home for burning gas, churning odometers, and mornings, noons, and nights spent on hard metal bleacher seats pretending there's nowhere else they'd rather be.

This book is dedicated to those I love who paid that price in order for me to follow my dream to the Major Leagues: my wonderful wife, Jill; my sons Brett and Ryan and my daughters Brooke and Ashley; as well as my parents, Bill and Sandy Olson, and my sister, Tammi Crampton.

Thanks to all of you, with love, for being co-MVPs of my team.

Gregg Olson

There is a well-worn saying that if you've got a thousand hours and quarts of blood to shed, anyone can write a book. Vowels and consonants are formidable foes and juggling them to tell a good story is often a lonely but noble pursuit.

Special thanks all those who inspire me, including my girls, Bonnie and Gracie, and everyone who has ever smelled the leather and pounded the mitt or yelled, "Hey, batter, batter!" from the stands. And to all my pals in the nearly famous No Bats Baseball Club, especially J. J. Gottsch, who, during our search for the perfect name, suggested, "Hey Blue! Bend Over and Use Your Good Eye!"

What a great game this is.

Ocean Palmer

Table of Contents

Acknowledgments

A tip of the cap to all the great baseball men who helped make this collection possible. Forty Hall of Famers, All-Stars, former players, writers, and umpires contributed. The variety of what they shared is phenomenal.

In alphabetical order these men include: Jim Abbott, Larry Andersen, Bruce Benedict, Bob Boone, Chris Bosio, Jeff Brantley, George Brett, Mike Cameron, Gary Carter, Tony Clark, Will Clark, Doug DeCinces, Rob Dibble, Doug Flynn, George Frazier, Jim Fregosi, Brian Giles, Goose Gossage, Mark Grace, Mark Gubicza, Jack Howell, Rex Hudler, Tim Hudson, Ferguson Jenkins, Eric Karros, Mike Krukow, Mark Lemke, Gary Matthews, Ed Montague, Jim Palmer, Jamie Quirk, Tracy Ringolsby, Brooks Robinson, Cookie Rojas, Mike Scott, Joe Simpson, Don Sutton, Ralph Terry, and Robin Ventura.

Dozens more legends wait in the wings. We are already hard at work on volume two and look forward to properly thanking those contributing stars next season.

Another doff of the cap goes to Gina Hardin, daughter of former Oriole pitcher Jim Hardin. Jim died in a tragic plane crash in Key West on March 11, 1991. The day before he had hosted co-author Ocean Palmer for a private round of golf at Mayacoo Lakes Country Club in West Palm Beach, where Jim was the reigning club champion. Jim spent much of that round talking about life after baseball, his loving wife, Susan, and his three children: Gina, J. J. (James Junior), and infant son Michael.

Jim pitched for the Orioles, Yankees, and Braves during his six seasons in the Majors (1967-1972) but too many hard sliders shredded his shoulder and arm trouble abruptly ended his career. His cumulative record was 43-32, including 18 wins by September 1 for Earl Weaver and the 1968 Orioles. His ERA that season was 2.51, just a nudge above his career best 2.21, which Jim posted during his 8-3 rookie season.

Jim loved his time in the Majors. When asked about it he used to say, "We got to play baseball!"

When we were searching for the perfect name for the book, Gina volunteered what her dad often said. We loved it, with her permission borrowed Jim's phrase, and titled the book accordingly.

We thank Gina, and her late father, for their friendship, support, and enduring love of the game.

Introduction

❖ **Gregg Olson**

Every baseball player has a story, and the idea for *We Got to Play Baseball* came when several of us got together during a celebrity golf tournament at Camp Lejeune, North Carolina.

During the event's final evening, many former players and some of the celebrities were sitting around telling stories. One of the wives was laughing just as loud as we were and said, "Someone should write these stories down." Ding ding! The idea of assembling a collection of favorite stories from men I'd played with and against was born.

I got home from the trip and called my friend Ocean Palmer and asked him what he thought. Ocean has written books and screenplays, and I thought he would be an enormous help. How I came to know him is a story in itself.

We first connected through the mail when I was playing my rookie season in Baltimore. Each week I got a letter from this guy who would never send a card or anything he wanted autographed.

To put it in perspective, I got exactly one letter a week without cards, photos, or baseballs to sign. He'd send supportive notes or doctored "In the Bleachers" cartoons, simply to give me a laugh.

He did it for years. A few seasons into my career, after my Orioles were involved in a bench-clearing brawl against the Seattle Mariners, he shipped me a package. Inside was a pair of boxing gloves signed and personalized to me by Angelo Dundee, Muhammad Ali's longtime boxing trainer. The gist of the message was, "For a fighter, you're a pretty good pitcher."

As time passed, I recognized his handwriting and looked forward to his letters. He had no agenda other than to make me laugh and boost my spirits. Throughout the ups and downs of a Major League career, especially for a pitcher with arm problems, that kind of support means a lot.

It was six years before we met. When I left the Orioles and went to spring training with the Atlanta Braves, we met up in spring training and went to the Florida Derby at Gulfstream Park. We bet the lock of the century and lost. We also played golf, and I had dinner at his home in Miami with his wife and daughter. We've been friends ever since, and now he's my co-author.

I'm a Midwesterner, born in Scribner, Nebraska and raised in Omaha. My father, Bill, is a nationally known baseball coach who shaped me into a Major Leaguer. I played baseball and football in high school with good success and decided to pitch in college rather than accept a scholarship to go to Nebraska and become a lineman.

I went to Auburn and pitched for three years. I was fortunate enough to be taken fourth overall in the June 1988 draft by the Baltimore Orioles and turned professional.

I made it to the Majors two months later and in 1989 was the team's closer. I had 27 saves and was voted American League Rookie of the Year, which means I'm the answer to a good baseball trivia question: What year did Ken Griffey, Jr. win Rookie of the Year?

The answer is he didn't. Griffey finished third in the balloting behind me and Tom Gordon. Ken went on to have a remarkable career, and I'm glad we have a story about him in the book; he was a superstar player who earned his way fair and square to Cooperstown. He's sure to go in the first year he's eligible, 2016.

I had a good fastball, but my money pitch was my curveball. Until I got hurt and bounced around the latter half of my career, I had a lot of success closing games. I had 217 saves, combined with three others to pitch a no-hitter and was lucky enough to make the All-Star team in 1990. Many of my teammates from that game (and many other All-Star games) contributed stories to our collection. Several are Hall of Famers.

Every story was told to me in person with the exception of Jim Fregosi's. When I asked Jim for one, he reached into his briefcase and handed me a copy of a magazine article with several. I liked one in particular and thought you would too, so we included it with his permission. All the rest I recorded and transcribed. Ocean did the rest.

Baseball players and fans share a very special bond. I hope you enjoy *We Got to Play Baseball* as much as I enjoyed hearing the stories my friends so willingly shared.

❖ Ocean Palmer

When Gregg called and spoke to me about the idea of putting together a collection of stories, I encouraged him to do it. I was happy to help; I love the game, and one of my earlier books was Searching for Tendulkar, a baseball travelogue detailing a remarkable 17-day trip across southern India spent teaching baseball to cricket coaches in a cricket-mad country.

For many years during Gregg's career, I stayed busy playing low-level amateur baseball all around the world, a goodwill ambassador who taught and spread a love for the game. I had nowhere near the skill it takes to compete at a level close to the men you'll read about. Regardless the length of a man's Major League career, simply getting to The Show takes an amazing amount of talent.

This book, we hope, is the next best thing to being there.

Baseball is a team game played by individuals—a basic truth at every level from Little League to the Major Leagues—and *We Got to Play Baseball* illustrates that, thanks to the tremendous array of stories Gregg collected.

He spoke with Hall of Famers, All-Stars, teammates, and opponents. Some of our contributors played for decades, others for only a few games. In addition to the players, Gregg also sat down with managers, coaches, umpires, and scouts—even an official scorer.

We Got to Play Baseball was a lot of fun to compile, research, and write, but for us its greatest meaning is what the book represents: a shared love of the game by the men who play it and the fans who cheer them on.

We hope you enjoy it.

1

George Frazier

Bombs over Boston

When I was with the Yankees, we were in Boston for a series against the Red Sox. A bunch of us got together and made a water balloon bomber. It required 25 feet of surgical tubing and six cones, similar to the funnels used to pour a can of oil into a car's crankcase. Tape it all together, punch the holes, and put it on there.

Ron Guidry is pitching for us the next day, so he's absent, but 24 of the 25-man Yankee roster are on the roof of the bank adjacent to our hotel. The bank is five stories high and connected to the downtown Sheraton Towers.

Getting there is easy. From our hotel, we simply have to take the elevator up from the lobby, crisscross over to the bank side, and climb the fire escape to the roof. No one says a word as we make our way through the Sheraton lobby with sacks and pillowcases full of beer and water balloons. We have five big garbage sacks full of water balloons and enough beer to eventually litter the bank rooftop with empty beer cans.

Bob Shirley is leaning on the edge, looking down on the streets below and spotting. Goose (Gossage) and I grab hold of the bomber's ends. Graig Nettles is the shooter. We are firing these water balloons off the roof from five stories up and they are flying almost four hundred feet. They explode in the street; people jump back and wonder, "What the heck is going on?"

Shirley suddenly points and orders, "Five steps left."

Me, Goose, and Nettles move five steps to our left, take aim, and fire. Nettles hits a lady in the head. She drops. And the way she goes down, we think she's dead. Her husband quickly grabs her and drags her away, into an alley.

We can still see them so we cease-fire to watch. Once she starts coming around and starts moving, we know she's okay. We resume with the beer drinking and bombing.

Goose tires of holding the end of the bomber, so he hands it off to Jay Howell. After a few bombs with Howell in there, Goose says matter-of-factly, "We're done."

We look back behind us, and there are 25 of Boston's finest coming over the walls with guns drawn.

Graig Nettles looks at me and says, "I just sent my kid to reform school in Montana. Now I'm going to get arrested for shooting water balloons off a bank in Boston."

I look at Nettles and say, "You deserve to be in jail."

The police thought we were robbing the bank. Our defense was straightforward: "We're the Yankees."

Their response was straightforward, too: "Get off the roof."

At about 2:00 a.m., we're in a nearby bar called Lettucehead, and I decide to return to the bank roof to retrieve my launcher. I go get it and return to the bar, where I convince Shane Rawley and Dave Righetti to go with me. We go back outside and plan to resume firing. We walk into the middle of the quiet intersection, I'm laying flat on my back in launch mode, and we're going to shoot at the first person who walks out of the bar.

The door shoves open, and out step Nettles and Gossage. They spot us and scream not to shoot, but it's too late; they're already in the crosshairs.

Well, I am already set on letting this balloon go, but Rawley steps back, which changes the angle and tension and causes me to fire a balloon that zooms like a nasty slider right into the bar's picture window, which explodes.

The last thing I need is to meet another policeman, so I hurry inside the bar and peel off $600 to the owner to replace the window. Even with the cash, he's still pissed. He has to hang around until someone can come and replace the window. None of us are welcome back in that bar for quite awhile.

I kept the launcher and stowed it in a safe place. A few years later, I'm with the Indians, and we are playing in Milwaukee.

Rene Lachemann is managing their ballclub, and he's having a tough time. They aren't winning, so his team is taking extra batting practice at three o'clock.

Bert Blyleven and I hike up to the upper deck of Milwaukee County Stadium. Bert is my spotter; he's sitting nearby, pretending to read a magazine, and acting like he's killing time doing nothing.

After I fire a balloon, he gives me new coordinates. "No," he says. "Two more feet to the left, Fraz."

I'm shooting and shooting, down onto the field, and the players can't figure out where the bombs are coming from. Water balloons are exploding on the infield, the mound, and the outfield.

Blyleven suddenly interrupts. "Uh-oh," he says, "I think we're caught."

I look down, and all the Brewers are standing around the batting cage at home plate looking up our way. I load and fire three more balloons all at once. All three blast open on top of the batting cage, drenching everybody.

Lachemann screams, "That's enough! We're done, alright, we're done!"

I'm thinking, "The hell you are," and fire five more.

About an hour later, I get a message from Brewers catcher Ted Simmons: he wants the launcher. I take it over and give it to him.

Not long after, Teddy's two sons, John and Matthew, have the police called on them in downtown Milwaukee because they're launching water balloons off a balcony.

As far as I know, Simmons still has the launcher. But I made a new one, and now I'm training my grandkids how to use it. I must keep the tradition going.

❖ George Frazier

George was a right-handed relief pitcher who pitched for 10 years in the Major Leagues, primarily in middle relief and in late-game situations. George pitched for five teams, among them the Yankees (1981-83) and the Indians (part of 1984). His career record was 35-43. He finished 193 of 415 career appearances and had 29 saves.

❖ Graig Nettles

Graig spent half of his 22-year career with the Yankees and made six All-Star teams, his last with the San Diego Padres in 1985. A solid-fielding third baseman, Nettles played in 2,700 Major League games and was widely respected for hitting with power. With a career slugging percentage of .421, Graig hit 390 home runs and drove in 1,314. A career .248 hitter, Graig's durability and everyday reliability enabled him to amass 2,225 hits and score 1,193 runs.

Nettles played in 13 postseason series and hit five home runs in 53 games. He was on the winning team in two of five World Series, winning back to back with the Yankees in 1977-78. He was also awarded a Gold Glove for his defensive work during both championship seasons.

❖ Bert Blyleven

Born in the Netherlands and raised in Southern California, Blyleven and his famous curveball fluttered to a 287-250 lifetime record, with 3,701 strikeouts. The durable right-hander started and finished 242 of 685 lifetime starts, more than one-third of every game he pitched over 22 seasons. Seventeen times he won 10 or more games and 13 seasons saw Bert complete 10 or more starts.

He was dominating for Minnesota in 1973, going 20-17 with 25 complete games in 40 starts and throwing 9 of his 60 career shutouts. Bert pitched 325 innings that season and finished with a sparkling 2.52 earned run average—one of 10 seasons his ERA was below 3.00.

Blyleven made two All-Star teams and was a clutch performer in the postseason, going 5-1 in five series. He pitched and helped win both World Series his teams played in, first with the Pittsburgh Pirates in 1979 against the Baltimore Orioles and again eight years later with the Minnesota Twins versus the St. Louis Cardinals.

Although Bert gave up 430 home runs during his career, he never managed to hit one. He went to the plate 514 times and finished with 52 singles and 7 doubles.

Voting support for Bert's induction to the Baseball Hall of Fame continued to grow in the years following retirement. Nineteen years after finishing his career with the California Angels, Bert earned enshrinement in the class of 2011, joining Roberto Alomar and front office executive Pat Gillick.

❖ Ted Simmons

An eight-time All-Star during his 21-year career, Ted was a switch-hitting catcher and first baseman who played for three teams: the St. Louis Cardinals, Milwaukee Brewers, and Atlanta Braves. During a three-season stretch with the Cardinals Simmons caught a remarkable 153, 141, and 154 games—448 of 486 games played (92.2%). Seven times he hit .300 or more and finished with an outstanding career average of .285. He was honored with a NL Silver Slugger award in 1980 while with the Cardinals.

With a watchful eye, Simmons was tough to strike out. He had nearly 10,000 Major League plate appearances and walked far more often (855) than he fanned (694).

Ted finished with nearly 2,500 hits and 1,400 runs batted in. He made it to one World Series, 1982, but as fate would have it, his Brewers lost to the team that originally signed him as a first round draft choice (tenth overall) in the 1965 draft—the St. Louis Cardinals.

2

Chris Bosio

Umpire
Angel Hernandez

I'm the pitching coach for the Tampa Bay Rays, and Victor Zambrano is pitching for us. Victor is one of those wild fast-ball pitchers who is either going to strike out 10 or walk 10.

Victor a having a walk-10 day against New York and the Yankees go up 5-0. The drums are beating loudly in the Bronx. Lou Piniella, our manager, sends me out to the mound.

"Go talk to this guy," he says. "Settle him down."

I go out to the mound, taking my time and stalling to get our guy in the bullpen a chance to get going.

Angel Hernandez is the home plate umpire and gives me a little time to talk with Victor but not a lot. Angel walks out to speed us up.

As Angel approaches, I tell Victor, "Victor, I'm going to tell this guy a joke."

Victor doesn't understand; he was kind of in a place of his own.

Angel arrives on the mound, and I start telling him a joke about Bill and Hillary Clinton going to Bosnia, weaving in the Clintons and Vice-President Al Gore. The joke's basic premise is that one of them has to go to Bosnia; none wants to but one of them must.

It's a bit off-colored but has a really good punch line.

I get to the end of the joke, deliver the punch line, and Angel throws me out of the game. He says he doesn't find it funny.

I go back to our dugout, and Lou asks me what happened.

"I told him my Bill Clinton joke," I said, "and he threw me out."

"He did what?" Lou being Lou, he bolts out of the dugout and runs out onto the field to talk to Angel.

"Angel," he says, "you can't throw a guy out of the game for telling a joke."

Hernandez looks at Lou. "Yes, I can," he says. "I thought the joke was very offensive."

❖ Angel Hernandez

Born in Havana, Cuba, Angel Hernandez has been a much talked about Major League umpire for twenty years. Throughout Angel's career, his on-field reputation has been shaped by some erratic calls and on-the-field confrontations with players, coaches, and managers.

Hernandez is the only umpire ever to throw a guy out of a ballgame for singing "Take Me Out to the Ballgame." In 2001, he tossed Chicago Bears defensive end Steve McMichael at Wrigley Field because Angel felt McMichael took a verbal jab at his umpiring skills during comments McMichael made after being introduced as the Cubs' guest singer.

❖ Chris Bosio

Chris Bosio pitched 11 seasons in the Majors, the first seven for the Milwaukee Brewers, the final four for the Seattle Mariners. A right-handed starter, Chris won 94 Big League games. He won 10 or more in a season five times and over a two-year span with the Brewers was 30-16, winning nearly half of his 65 starts. Bosio was a reliable and durable pitcher; he averaged nearly seven innings per start.

El Paso was Bosio's 1985 minor league AA Texas League season, one of six stops en route to reaching the Majors in 1986. After retiring, Chris has continued to work in baseball as a coach and scout. He currently works for the Milwaukee Brewers.

3

Doug DeCinces

Hey, Earl!
Who's on First?

This story involves Oriole manager Earl Weaver and goes way back to when I was playing for him in 1977. We are playing the Chicago White Sox, who have the bases loaded and Jim Essian coming to the plate. Essian is a journeyman catcher once traded for Dick Allen and Johnny Oates, who I later also played for.

Earl walks out to the mound, takes the ball from the pitcher, and waves in left-hander Scott McGregor. This is early in Scott's career when he is a reliever. When Scott gets to the mound, Earl hands him the ball and says, "Walk this guy and get the next hitter."

Scott is a left-handed pitcher, and the on-deck hitter is left-handed, and that lefty/lefty matchup is what Earl wants.

Rick Dempsey is our catcher. He looks at each base and takes inventory. Dempsey tells Earl, "The bases are loaded."

Earl snaps back, "No, they're not, Dempsey, shut up."

I'm playing third base that day, standing on the mound listening to these guys argue about strategy. So I look around, too.

Dempsey's right. The White Sox have a runner on every base.

I chime in, "No, Earl, they are loaded."

Earl looks at first, looks at second, looks at third, and says, "Oh shit." He walks off the mound and stalks back to the dugout, leaving Dempsey and McGregor just standing there. It's up to them to figure out what to do.

The game resumes, and Essian hits a bloop double down the left field line, knocking in two runs, and we end up losing that game.

If a fan is ever curious about what a mound discussion involves, now you know. Sometimes we all get together just to figure out how many guys are on base.

❖ Doug DeCinces

Born in Burbank, right-handed hitting third baseman Doug DeCinces was a third-round draft choice of the Baltimore Orioles in 1970 and reached the Majors three years later at the age of 22. He played 15 seasons and finished third in the American League Most Valuable Player voting in 1982, his first of 6 seasons with the California Angels. Doug had career highs that season in doubles (42), home runs (30), runs batted in (97), and batting average (.301). He was awarded a Silver Slugger that year and made the All-Star team the next.

❖ Earl Weaver

Born and raised in St. Louis, diminutive and hot-tempered, Earl Weaver found his fame chain-smoking and stalking the Baltimore Orioles dugout for 17 seasons. Earl was a winner, going 1,480-1,060 for his career while leading the O's to four American League pennants and the 1970 World Series championship.

Under Earl, the Orioles made it to the Series three years in a row, from 1969 through 1971, losing to the Miracle Mets, defeating Cincinnati' Big Red Machine, and losing to the We Are Family Pittsburgh Pirates. During that span, the club won 109, 108, and 101 regular season games.

Earl was enshrined in Cooperstown in 1996, voted in by the Veterans Committee along with perfect game and double-no hit pitcher Jim Bunning, 19th-century manager Ned Hanlon, and 1920s-30s Negro League left-handed pitching legend (Big) Bill Foster.

4

Mark Gubicza

Ape

Kevin Appier was a workhorse right-handed starting pitcher for the Royals and was famous on our team for three reasons: he could really pitch, you never wanted him to be on the hill on getaway day, and he was perhaps baseball's ultimate clean freak. I don't know if the word germophobic captures him perfectly, but Ape was one of a kind; his life is an all-out war against bacteria. The man has a fastidious need to be clean.

As good as Ape was, we never wanted him to pitch on getaway day because he threw so many pitches. He battled everyone, from his first hitter to his last. Plus he struck out a lot of guys. These translate into long games, which are the archenemy when you're in a hurry to get out of town.

When Ape threw on getaway day, and we factored in his customary 30-minute post-game shower, day could turn into night, and night could morph into early morning. Complicating things further was another one of his quirks: Ape insisted that his half-hour shower must be taken under one, specific showerhead. If someone else was using it, he would wait.

One day we got a screwdriver and removed the entire showerhead from the wall. Kevin goes into shower, and, as only Ape can scream, wails, "OH NO, where's my showerhead!"

Without his showerhead, he would not shower. And if he won't shower, we can't leave. We are forced to confront a perplexing and unexpected stalemate: it's getaway day, Appier won't shower, and even if he caves and decides he will, he'll be in there scrubbing for thirty minutes at least.

We're scrambling and decide to bite the bullet, give up the prank, and put the damn showerhead back into the wall so Ape can shower, and we can get out of town.

My favorite Ape story happened when one of the guys threw a wet towel on the chair in front of his locker. Appier exits the shower after his normal thirty minutes. He's just ahead of me, so I get to watch vintage Ape in action.

Approaching his locker, he spies the wet towel on his chair and stops, dead in his tracks. He stares at the towel and turns a very pale shade. Ape turns and beelines back into the shower and stands under his showerhead for another thirty minutes.

Thankfully, baseball players aren't eternally cruel. During Ape's second shower, whoever put the wet towel on his chair took it off and tossed it in the hamper. Kevin only showered for one-hour that day.

He was such an easy target that one thing I liked to do was grab a Q-tip, swab out my inner ear, and put it on Ape's chair.

He wouldn't even go near the chair. He would get one of the clubbies to move the chair and bring him a new one.

Kevin Appier was a classic, an all-time, one of a kind, priceless teammate. He was a fun guy, good to be around, pure entertainment. The rest of us joked that with Ape around, we didn't need TV to pass the time. We'd just watch him.

Ape even had dugout routines for the days he started. His most important ritual was his cup toss. He would drink a cup of water and flip the cup to his right.

We would purposely stand there, in his way, blocking him from tossing.

Ape would wait us out. He'd hold that empty cup until we moved. Then he'd toss it. Appier had mega-routines. The cup toss was merely one.

For all his quirks and peccadilloes, Kevin Appier was one heck of a Major League pitcher. There we many days and nights where the rest of us watch him work and think, "Man, maybe we need to start flipping cups too."

❖ Kevin Appier

Kansas City's first round draft choice in 1987, Appier was a starter throughout his career and played the first 10 of his 16 Major League seasons for the Royals. He had 115 of his 169 wins for Kansas City and made the 1995 All-Star team. He won 11 or more games 10 times. His best season was 1993, when he went 18-8 with a 2.56 ERA. Although he never made it to the postseason with the Royals, he reached the World Series late in his career with the Anaheim Angels, who beat the San Francisco Giants in 2002 in seven games to win the championship.

❖ Mark Gubicza

Six-feet-six righty Mark Gubicza was a mainstay on the Kansas City starting rotation for most of his 14-year Major League career. Twice an All-Star, Gubicza finished third in the 1988 Cy Young voting after going 20-8 with a 2.70 ERA, eight complete games, and four shutouts. At age 22, he started and beat Toronto 5-3 on the road in game six of the American League Championship Series. The Royals used just six pitchers in their seven-game World Series win over the St. Louis Cardinals, so the pivotal win in the ALCS was Mark's only postseason appearance.

5

3 points of view: Larry Andersen, Joe Simpson, and Tracy Ringolsby

Mr. Jell-O

❖ Larry Andersen's View

In 1982, I was on the Seattle Mariners, and Rene Lachemann was my manager. We were in Chicago to play the White Sox and Lee Pelekoudas (later to become Mariners GM) was the traveling secretary.

Lee got a key to Lachemann's room suite and Richie Zisk, Joe Simpson, and I borrowed the key from him. The three of us went to the store and bought 16 boxes of cherry Jell-O. We were going to get a dozen boxes but remembered their advertising campaign: There's always room for Jell-O. So we grabbed more.

There were two bathrooms in Lache's suite, so we dumped 8 boxes of Jell-O into each toilet. Then we twice filled his trashcan with ice, emptied one load into each commode, and mixed together the ice and Jell-O.

Satisfied with our chemistry project, we pretty much— I wouldn't say annihilate or destroy—moved everything in the suite. We pulled the mattress off Lache's bed, carried it into the bathroom, and stood it in the tub. We turned all the chairs upside down and unplugged all the electronics.

Then we toilet-papered the entire suite. When finished, we stepped back and studied our work. We were quite proud. Anything we could think of, we did. Our final move before quietly exiting was removing the speaking device from the phone. We wanted this to be a personal journey for Lache and saw no need for him to be able to call for help.

As we are redecorating, Lache is out on Rush Street having a few cocktails. He ambles back to the hotel, makes his way to the suite, and wants to crash. It's probably two or three in the morning. He walks in and flips on the light switch. The room stays dark; we have removed all the light bulbs. In the dark, Lache manages his way to the room telephone, finds it, and calls Richie Zisk's room.

Richie answers but can't hear Lache because we removed the microphone piece from his phone. Richie assumes it's Lache but can't hear him and hangs up. Richie's phone rings again.

Richie answers immediately with, "I don't know who this is, but I don't appreciate you calling. I have a game tomorrow." Then he hangs up.

By now Lache realizes that whomever he calls can't hear him; he has to find a mouthpiece for the phone.

We go to the ballpark the next day, and Lache is livid. He threatens us with the FBI, fingerprint tests, and lie detector tests—pretty much everything except waterboarding and bamboo shoots under our fingernails.

We're just laughing, all three of us playing it straight, and Lache can't figure out whom to blame.

One of the guys on the White Sox, outfielder Tom Paciorek, had been with us the year before but had gotten traded. Lache sees Paciorek at the park and tells him what happened. Lache is guessing. He blames Paciorek but isn't sure the culprit isn't someone on his own ballclub. His prime suspect is Richie Zisk.

Word gets out, the story gets legs, and there is an article in the newspaper where Lache is blaming Paciorek or intimating that at the very least, Paciorek is somehow involved.

Paciorek's mother takes offense. She calls Lache and says her son would never do any such thing.

From that point on, every time we go to a new city, Lee Pelekoudas would have molds of Jell-O, balloons, and whipped cream waiting in Lache's hotel room whenever he checked in. Accompanying the gift baskets are welcomes notes from Mr. Jell-O.

Then we get legendary Mariner broadcaster Dave Niehaus involved. We get a bunch of guys talking about the caper and convince Dave to take Lache aside and tell him he

(Dave) has a tape of us confessing. Dave has no such thing; he never turned on his recorder.

Dave plays along. He goes to Lache and says that he has some information for him. Lache wants it immediately. Dave explains he needs his recorder for the postgame show but as soon as the game is over and he's finished with his interviews, he'll bring it over and play what he's got.

During batting practice, Lache strolls out into the outfield where I am shagging fly balls.

"I know who did it," he says. "I know you're in on it."

I'm not convinced. I look at him and disagree. "No you don't."

"I have proof."

"No, you don't."

"I'll bet you one hundred bucks I do."

I take the bet.

Well, Richie Zisk is that night's star of the game, and Richie tells Niehaus not to give Lache any info. Having everybody in on it, including our announcer, makes the Mr. Jell-O caper that much more fun.

Niehaus enters the clubhouse just as I'm asking Lache for my hundred bucks. Lache sees Niehaus coming and says, "Get your hundred ready. Niehaus," he calls with a wave, "come here!"

Dave (Niehaus) walks over and looks uneasily at Lache. He shakes his head and says, "You're not going to believe what happened."

Lache looks puzzled.

"It got erased," says Niehaus. "I accidentally erased it."

Lache goes off, angrily barking, "Those blankety-blanks got to you, didn't they?"

Niehaus insists it's an honest mistake.

Our next road city is New York, and there I have custom newspapers printed with a big, bold headline that reads JELL-O -GATE TAPES LOST—LACHE BAFFLED!

I have the fake newspapers posted all around the Yankee Stadium visitors' clubhouse. Lache walks in, sees the papers, and gets the red-ass. He is really mad.

The gag plays on. Every chance we have to do something, we take. For three months, we pour salt in the wound.

At our end season-ending team party, Joe Simpson goes and gets three large brown paper grocery bags. He colors each like a Jell-O box.

Richie Zisk, Joe Simpson, and me—the three culprits—wear the bags over our heads.

Lache can't tell who is under the bags, nor is he allowed to look around to inventory who else is in the room. He has to stand and face us, a What's My Line type of guessing game. With no other clues, Lache had to figure out who truly is Mr. Jell-O.

From the night the prank began, to the length of time it lasted, to the Jell-O in the beer cans—I don't think we held back on anything. Everything we could think of to mess with Lache, we did.

He is blaming Bill Caudill, then Al Cowens, but is clueless and has no idea. Caudill is certainly a likely suspect. We had already nicknamed him "the Inspector" after he decided to inspect our bats for unused hits and threw bats away if they looked empty with none remaining. Once Caudill entered a game in relief wearing a half-shaved beard. Another time he stole the keys to the bullpen golf cart during a pre-game ceremony—delaying the game because the cart was stranded along the foul line. He was an All-Star in 1984, but his career ended after breaking his hand at 30. He was super-agent Scott Boras' first client and works for Boras today. But to Lache, all Caudill was a prime suspect.

I have no idea why Lache suspected Cowens. All Al ever did was ground back to the pitcher and run to the mound instead of first base, seeking a bit of manly-man revenge for an earlier incident (Ed Farmer broke Al's jaw with a pitch). What's wrong with that?

Time is the test of all great achievements and the Mr. Jell-O Caper might very well be the best and gutsiest prank that I've ever been involved with.

So far.

❖ Joe Simpson's Take

In 1982, I was playing for the Seattle Mariners, and Rene Lachemann was our manager. He was the best, most fun manager I ever played for. Lache made it fun to come to the park.

We had an off day in Chicago. With help from our traveling secretary, Richie Zisk and Larry Andersen got a key to Lache's suite.

While others were entertaining Lache in the hotel bar at the Chicago Westin— "others" being defined as noted baseball writer Tracy Ringolsby—the three of us went up to Lache's room.

Larry Andersen had gotten some cherry Jell-O, mixed it with a bucket of ice, and poured the stuff into both of Lache's toilets.

It gelled.

We stripped Lache's bedding and shoved it in the closet. Then we moved all the furniture into the bathroom; it was full to the point that Lache wouldn't be able to open the door.

The only things we didn't terrorize were his clothes; those we put neatly inside the dresser. The final thing we did before leaving was remove the speaking microphone piece from the room telephone. That way Lache couldn't call down to find out what the heck happened.

The next day we arrive at the ballpark, old Comiskey, and written on the chalkboard is, "$500 reward for information leading to the arrest of Mr. Jell-O."

Then we have to sit through a team meeting and hear that the hotel is upset. There are damages (they say), and management plans to get fingerprints. Larry, Richie, and I look at each other thinking, "Uh oh."

Bill Caudill, our closer, had a great sense of humor and character. He wasn't even involved but spoke up to help smokescreen us.

Caudill pipes up with, "You know, Lache, I saw you over there talking to your buddy Tony La Russa (manager of the

White Sox). I saw you concocting all this. You're going to have cops come over here to try to strong-arm everybody."

Lache's shoulders slump when Caudill calls him out. This unexpected alibi was music to our ears. We knew right away we were okay.

Throughout the rest of the season Richie Zisk would anonymously send Lache little presents from Mr. Jell-O, delivered by gift shops to Lache's office, things like baskets of Jell-O adorned with dancing helium balloons.

This went on all year, with Lache trying to investigate who Mr. Jell-O really is. It became a great, good-natured, and fun way to promote camaraderie on the team.

Lache played along until the end of the season, when we had our team party and let him try to guess Mr. Jell-O. He guessed two of the three guys involved.

And now he knows the third.

❖ Tracy Ringolsby Chimes In

The players got announcer Dave Niehaus involved with the Mr. Jell-O caper. He (Niehaus) approached Lache (Mariner's manager Rene Lachemann) and said, "Hey Lache, I know who Mr. Jell-O is. I was holding a recorder down by my side, and I heard Joe Simpson talking about Mr. Jell-O."

Niehaus and Lache go and listen to the tape behind home plate at Memorial Stadium. Lache hears Simpson on tape: "Yeah, I know who Mr. Jell-O is. Lache will kick himself when he finds out who it is."

Niehaus goes upstairs to the press box while Lache goes out to the field for warm-ups. Lache walks right up to Simpson during stretching and asks, "Do you have any idea who Mr. Jell-O is?"

Simpson shakes his head. "No," he says. "I haven't got any idea at all."

"You liar! I know you know who Mr. Jell-O is!"

"Lache, I got no idea who Mr. Jell-O is."

"I'll bet you $100 that you know who Mr. Jell-O is."

"How are you going to prove it?"

"Come with me."

They go into the clubhouse, and Lache calls Niehaus down from the press box, telling him to bring his recorder. When Niehaus arrives, Lache has him push play on the recorder. Niehaus does, but the tape is blank. There's nothing on it.

We fly to New York. When we arrive at Yankee Stadium the next day, plastered all over the clubhouse are newspapers with the screaming headline: JELLOGATE TAPES BLANK, LACHE BAFFLED!

The team arrives home from the trip, and Mr. Jell-O has become a big deal in the Seattle papers; everyone's guessing, but no one can figure out who Mr. Jell-O is. Here's how bad it got: the coaches went out for a drink at a local lounge and were served a bowl of Jell-O.

Then the staff has a coaches meeting in Lache's office— Billy Plummer, Dave Duncan, and Lache. They grab beers out of Lache's refrigerator, pop them open to get a big swig of beer, and the cans are full of Jell-O. The culprit was a guy who dropped off the team's road trip equipment back at the stadium. He had no idea who Mr. Jell-O was, but he had read and heard so much about Mr. Jell-O he wanted to get involved. While the club was out of town on its road trip, he and his wife punctured pinholes in the bottom of the beer can and drained all the beer out. They re-filled the cans with Jell-O mix, taped the pinholes shut, and put the cans of Jell-O beer back in Lache's refrigerator to gel.

It kept going like that the whole year. For example, we go back to Baltimore, back to the Cross Keys Hotel. Lache checks into the hotel, goes to his room, and flips on the light. Waiting to greet him is a big, silver tureen full of Jell-O.

Unbelievable.

* * *

❖ Rene Lachemann

A catcher for portions of three years in the Major Leagues, Lache has held many Major League coaching jobs and has

managed three Big League teams: Seattle Mariners, Milwaukee Brewers, and Florida Marlins. He skippered a fourth, the
Chicago Cubs, for one game as an interim manager in 2002.

The son of a hotel chef, Lache was a batboy for the Los
Angeles Dodgers and signed a pro contract with the Kansas City Athletics in 1964, where his teammates and close
friends included Tony La Russa and Dave Duncan.

Lache played more than half of the 1965 season, hitting
nine home runs in 92 games. He is a very popular baseball
man, long considered "a player's manager."

❖ Larry Andersen

Larry pitched in the Majors for 17 years but was in Seattle
for only two, 1981-82. A middle reliever, he was 3-3 with
six saves in 81 games while pitching for Lache. Larry arrived in Seattle via a trade from Pittsburgh, where he was the
"player to be named later" in a deal for Odell Jones.

❖ Richie Zisk

A 13-year Major League veteran, Zisk spent the first half of
his career with the Pittsburgh Pirates before playing for the
Chicago White Sox, Texas Rangers, and Seattle Mariners.
Zisk's Major League debut came when he replaced legendary Hall of Famer Roberto Clemente in right field during
the eighth inning of a blowout win over the Cubs late in the
1971 season.

A solid hitter with good power, Richie's career batting
average was .287. He clubbed 207 home runs and hit for the
cycle during a win over the San Francisco Giants at Candlestick Park.

A two-time All-Star, Richie batted cleanup for the American League during the 1978 game in San Diego, and earned
American League Comeback Player of the Year honors in
1981, batting .311 with 16 homers for the Seattle Mariners.

❖ Joe Simpson

Joe was a left-handed first baseman and outfielder with nine seasons in the Big Leagues. He was a light-hitting, part-time player with a career .242 average. He played for three teams—Los Angeles Dodgers, Seattle Mariners, and Kansas City Royals.

With the Royals, Joe twice came in to pitch relief. He pitched a total of three innings, facing fifteen hitters and giving up but one run, four hits, and a pair of walks. He also struck out a batter.

❖ Bill Caudill

Right-hander Bill Caudill pitched nine seasons in the Majors, primarily in relief. During his four busiest seasons, he averaged nearly 70 appearances with earned run averages of 2.19, 2.71, 2.35, and 2.99. He saved 106, including a career high 36 with Oakland in 1984, a season in which he represented the A's in the All-Star game.

❖ Tracy Ringolsby

Tracy Ringolsby is an esteemed baseball writer who has covered the sport since 1976. A former president of the Baseball Writers Association of America, Tracy was presented with the BWAA's highest honor, the prestigious J. G. Taylor Spink Award at baseball's 2005 Hall of Fame induction ceremony in Cooperstown. Spink Award honorees are eligible for selection to the Hall of Fame's Veterans Committee panels that elect non-players and players whose careers began before 1943.

Spink Award winners are a small, esteemed fraternity that includes only the very best of America's baseball writers.

6

Cookie Rojas

The Legend of Moe Drabowsky

Moe Drabowsky was an excellent pitcher for the Baltimore Orioles. He also pitched for Kansas City. Moe was what you could call a Hall of Fame prankster. Wherever he was, he always played practical jokes. He was really good at it. Moe fooled everybody.

When Moe and I were teammates in Kansas City, we played in old Municipal Stadium. The dugouts were not like they are now, protected by fences. They were open, down the left and right field lines, and set back from the field.

I was new to the team. I had just been traded by the Cardinals to Kansas City, and we were going to play the Oakland A's. Alvin Dark was their manager.

I always got to the ballpark early. On this particular day, even though I was early, Moe was already there.

I went down to sit on our bench. Moe was walking the opposite direction, away from our dugout. He was carrying a large package.

Moe walked into Oakland's dugout, opened up the jumbo water container that sat atop the coolers in those days, and poured the contents of his package into the open neck of the water bottle. Then he replaced the jug back in its normal position atop the cooler.

Game time rolls around, and Moe walks into our dugout with a pair of binoculars. He stands there, raises the binoculars to his eyes, and scans across the opposite side of the field.

I ask, "What are you doing?"

"I'm waiting for someone to get a drink of water."

He had poured three pounds of salt into their water cooler. Every time an Oakland player leaned over and got a drink, he would spit it onto the floor as fast as he could.

Moe was laughing his guts out.

❖ More Moe

Back then the dugouts used regular telephones. You could call directly anywhere. Moe was overjoyed to learn this. He could call any place he wanted.

Our game is getting ready to start, and again we're playing the A's. Their manager, Alvin Dark, walks back to the dugout after meeting with the umpires at home plate.

The umpire yells, "Play ball!"

Moe waits a couple minutes but not long. He picks up the telephone and calls the visiting bullpen.

He barks, "Get the left-hander up" and slams the phone down.

Seconds later a left-hander starts warming up in the Oakland bullpen.

There hasn't been a single pitch thrown in the game yet, and Oakland has a guy warming in the pen.

Alvin Dark happens to look down toward the bullpen and notices his left-hander warming up. Alvin screams toward the pen, yelling for the guy to sit down.

Moe waits another two or three minutes and calls the visiting bullpen. This time he tells them to get the right-hander up. Seconds later, the right-hander gets up in the bullpen and starts to get loose.

Alvin Dark looks down toward the bullpen again; this time sees a right-hander warming up and starts going bananas.

That was Moe Drabowsky. He was just unbelievable, all the funny things he did. God bless him, he passed away a few years ago. He was a great guy, a great joker, and a great friend.

And a very good pitcher, too.

❖ Cookie Rojas

Born in Havana, Cuba, Cookie Rojas played baseball over the objections of his father, who preferred he become a doctor. Cookie followed his heart and has been in baseball ever since.

Cookie played for 16 seasons and was a five-time All-Star. He was a sure-handed second baseman whose career batting average was .263. An outstanding contact hitter, throughout his long career he average one strikeout per 14 trips to the plate.

A long-time coach, scout, and broadcaster, Cookie managed the California Angels for a season, as well as the Florida Marlins.

❖ Moe Drabowsky

Born in Poland, Drabowsky's parents immigrated to Connecticut when Moe was three years old. He grew up there, threw a no-hitter in high school, and signed with the Cubs soon after. The tall righty's Major League playing career lasted 17 seasons.

Moe began as a starter but arm problems caused him to bounce around and eventually forced him to the bullpen, where he excelled.

In the 1966 World Series opener against the Los Angeles Dodgers, Drabowsky entered the game for the Orioles in the third inning and struck out eleven—including six men in a row—in a masterful winning performance that set the stage for three straight shutouts and Baltimore's impressive four-game sweep.

Drabowsky won the first game in Kansas City Royals history. He returned to the Orioles late in his career and pitched twice in the 1970 World Series when the Orioles defeated Cincinnati's Big Red Machine. He also gave up Stan Musial's 3,000th career hit and was the losing pitcher in Hall of Famer Early Wynn's 300th victory.

Ever the prankster, early in Drabowsky's career (with the Cubs), he was hit in the foot with a pitch. He convinced teammate Dick Drott to wheel him to first in a wheelchair, a stunt for which Drott was ejected. Moe was also respected as a master of the hotfoot; he gave one to baseball commissioner Bowie Kuhn during the Orioles' 1970 World Series celebration.

Drabowsky passed away in Little Rock, Arkansas in 2006. He was 70.

7

Gregg Olson

Jim Abbott: Troublemaker in Cuba

I had the great honor of playing for the United States three times during international competition. The first was in 1984 with Albert Belle and Jack McDowell on the Junior Olympic baseball team. We won a silver medal, losing to Cuba.

In 1987, I played for the Pan American team that also took silver to Cuba's gold.

The third time was for a few weeks with the 1988 US Olympic team; because of mononucleosis, I never got to finish the Olympic experience.

My favorite story stems from the 1987 Pan American team. We traveled to Cuba for a 10-day trip and played the Cuban National team seven times. We had a great team; my teammates included Jim Abbott, Tino Martinez, Ty Griffin, Joe Slusarski, Ed Sprague, Scott Servais, and Cris Carpenter.

Most of our games were played in Havana. We stayed in one of the city's finest hotels. Throughout our stay in Cuba, we also had people following us in and around the city. None of us was sure if they were tails, police, or federal officers.

To pass hotel time we played Kill the Man. Pitchers would try to catch a hitter alone while hitters would try to catch us pitchers alone. If caught, the victim absorbed a five-on-one pummeling (never any damage, mostly sore ribs).

We had other ways to entertain ourselves, too. Aside from punching teammates, we played a lot of cards and threw baseballs at each other in hotel rooms.

Jim Abbott was my roommate, and Abbott and I stayed up on the 14th floor. It is hot in Cuba in July, and windows are always open. We're playing a game that involves throwing

26

a baseball at each other. The game progresses, and the baseball flies out an open window.

The instant the balls sails out the window, we panic. We are in Cuba, always being watched, and have just thrown a missile out a window 14 stories up.

What do we do, look out the window and watch? No. Run down the hall to another player's room? No. Escape to the elevator and mingle in the lobby? No.

We do what all brave athletes do when faced with adversity: we hide under the beds.

In less than five minutes, there is a knock on the door.

We don't budge. We stay still.

After what seems like minutes, we're still under the beds, and there's a second knock. Whoever's knocking is not going away. I crawl out from under the bed to answer the door.

I open the door with one hand, my other arm raised over my head to surrender. I am fully prepared to point the finger at Abbott.

Standing there is a Havana police officer. Before I can rat out Abbott hiding under the bed, the policeman hands me the baseball and walks away.

The game resumes. Abbott is a dead duck beneath the bed.

❖ Jim Abbott

The pride of Flint, Michigan, Jim attended the University of Michigan from 1986-88 and was the eighth pick in the 1988 draft, chosen by the California Angels four spots behind Olson. Other notable Wolverines in the Majors have included Hall of Famers Charlie Gehringer and George Sisler, as well as future Hall of Famer Barry Larkin.

A great all-around athlete, Abbott was born without a right hand. Despite what for some may seem a handicap, Abbott excels at multiple sports and went on to pitch for 10 years in the Major Leagues. He won 87 games and threw 6 shutouts.

Abbott also was a successful hitter. He went 2-for-21 against Big League pitching and drove in three runs.

❖ Gregg Olson

During this trip to Havana, Olson was introduced to Fidel Castro, who expressed his admiration for Olson's devastating curveball.

8

Eric Karros

Roger & Tommy

We (the Dodgers) are playing in Cincinnati. Tommy Lasorda is our manager, and Tommy was known to catch a nap every now and then. It's a day game, and after batting practice, Tommy comes and lies down on the couch in his office. In moments, he's fast asleep.

Roger McDowell goes into the manager's office while Tommy is snoring and changes the clock. Game time is 1:05 p.m., and Roger moves the hands ahead so the time on the clock reads 1:20. He comes out of Tommy's office and clears everybody out of the clubhouse. The players scatter, and no one is left in the clubhouse except for the clubhouse workers.

The Reds' home field was the old Riverfront Stadium, and it was a long walk from the clubhouse through the tunnel and out to the visitors' dugout. One of the clubhouse guys goes in and urgently shakes Tommy awake.

"Skip," he says, "one of the guys is hurt out there, and they want to know what you want to do."

Tommy looks at the clock, is startled to have overslept, and starts screaming at the clubbie, "Why didn't you wake me up? Jesus Christ!"

Tommy rolls off his sofa and gets to his feet. He starts running, as only Tommy can do, down the steps, and then down the corridor. He's wearing his batting practice top, not his uniform. He's chugging as fast as he can. The clubhouse kid follows close behind.

"Get this thing off me," Tommy orders, pulling on his shirt. "I have to go manage." He finally reaches the top of the dugout steps, and we're all standing there. Tommy stops and looks around. All he can say is, "What the . . ."

He thought he had slept through the beginning of the game. Looking around and seeing us all laughing, it dawns on him the game hasn't even started.

For a while, Tommy is all bent out of shape about it, but after awhile, he accepts the joke and laughs about it.

We were glad about that. None of us wanted to do any extra running because of Roger McDowell.

❖ Eric Karros

Longtime Dodger first baseman Eric Karros played 14 years in the Majors, 12 with Los Angeles. He hit 20 homers his rookie season and was named National League Rookie of the Year ahead of Moises Alou and Tim Wakefield. A .268 life-time hitter, Karros his 284 homers and six times drove in over 100 runs. His best season was with the Dodgers in 1999, when he hit .304 with 40 doubles, 34 homers, and drove in 112 runs.

Eric made the postseason three times but never made it to the World Series. After losing consecutive Division Series in 1995-96 with the Dodgers, Eric was with the Cubs during their ill-fated 2003 "Bartman" playoff series against the Florida Marlins. Karros was as solid in the postseason as he was throughout the career, hitting .300 in four post-seasons.

❖ Roger McDowell

Drafted out of Bowling Green by the New York Mets in 1982, right-handed reliever Roger McDowell saved 159 games during 12 Major League seasons. He was a short relief specialist and finished his career with a 70-70 record and 3.30 ERA.

Roger was the winning pitcher for the Mets in game seven of the 1986 World Series, beating Calvin Schiraldi and Boston 8-5 to win the world championship. He appeared in five games that series and although 18 of 37 batters he faced reached base, only five Red Sox scored. In game seven, with the title on the line, McDowell safely navigated the seventh inning and got the ball to Mets closer Jesse Orosco to pitch the eighth and ninth.

Roger passed the time in mischievous ways, tossing lit firecrackers in the dugout and lighting hotfoots on unsuspecting teammates. He once joined an on-field mariachi band and also started wearing earrings after Reds owner Marge Schott mandated that her players couldn't.

Roger still enjoys life on the field and in the dugout. He is currently the Atlanta Braves' Major League pitching coach.

❖ Tom Lasorda

The pride of Norristown, Pennsylvania has spent six decades in baseball, all but one year with the Dodgers. He was voted into the Hall of Fame as a manager in 1997 in his first year of eligibility.

Tommy was drafted into professional baseball during World War II (1945) and briefly pitched in the minors until missing two years for military service. He returned to minor league ball in 1948 and struck out 25 men in a 15-inning game.

After a modest 3-year career as a Major League pitcher— he was 0-4 with a lifetime ERA of 6.48—Tommy quit playing and started coaching. After 15 years in the minors, Tommy replaced Walt Alston as Dodger manager in 1976. He managed the team for the next 3,138 games, winning 1,599 and two world championships, four pennants, and eight division titles in 20 years.

Lasorda managed four All-Star teams and nine Rookie of the Year winners, including four in a row: Eric Karros, Mike Piazza, Raul Mondesi, and Hideo Nomo.

After a mid-season heart attack in 1996, Tommy retired. He came out of retirement to manage the 2000 US Olympic team in Sydney, Australia. America won the gold medal, upsetting heavily favored Cuba.

Vocal and unabashed about his love of the game, Tommy Lasorda remains one of baseball's most recognizable personalities.

9

Don Sutton

Red Adams &
Harvey Kuenn

I'm not one who remembers stories real well, but one of my favorite meetings on the mound was with Red Adams, my pitching coach with the Dodgers.

One day I started against the Cubs and was having trouble getting out of the first inning. When a coach comes out for a visit, especially early, you're looking for words of wisdom that will help you get at least one guy out. Something positive you can use.

Red walks slowly from the dugout out to the mound, folds his arms across his chest, and asks, "Do you cheat?"

I emphatically answer, "No!"

"Might be a good time to start trying."

Red pivots back around and returns to the dugout, leaving me alone on the mound to ponder his suggestion.

Another time Red comes out when I'm pitching in Cincinnati. I have just walked in a run, the only time (I think) in my career I ever did.

Red has watched me walk three in a row. He calls time out, slowly ambles out to visit, and hikes up on the mound to see me.

He asks, "How's your fastball?"

"It's fine."

"How's your curveball?"

"My curveball is fine. What do you want?"

"How's your slider? It really looks good."

I said, "It is."

"Your changeup?"

32

"It's good," I said. "Everything is good." I frown at him, a bit frustrated with his line of questioning.

Red says, "Throw some of that crap for strikes." He turns around and walks away. That was it.

Red's meetings were often like that, short and to the point.

Another meeting that I'll always remember came after I was traded to the Milwaukee Brewers in 1983. I'd had about a total of five minutes with my new manager, Harvey Kuenn, and the exchange was a typical post-trade meeting: "Glad you're here, show up on time, give me your best, you know how to pitch . . . go."

We're in Boston, and I give up a two-run homer in the first, a two-run homer in the second, get two men out, and give up a double. I'm standing on the mound rubbing the baseball and see Harvey limping out to the mound. He'd had a severe blood clot problem in 1980, and now has a wooden leg, so it takes him awhile to get there.

He hikes up the mound and asks, "What's the score?"

"What?"

"What's the score?"

"It's 4-0 them."

"The way I figure it, them sonsabitches are down by five. Get that guy out." He limps back to the dugout, and we end up winning, 14-4.

❖ Don Sutton

Hall of Fame pitcher Don Sutton was signed as an amateur free agent by the Los Angeles Dodgers in 1964 and two years later began a 23-year career that produced a lifetime record of 324-256 with a 3.26 ERA and 3,574 strikeouts. Sutton threw 58 career shutouts, including a league-leading nine in 1972 when he went 19-9 with a 2.08 earned run average for the Dodgers. He spent 16 seasons with Los Angeles, getting 52 of his shutouts and 233 of his wins while starting for the Dodgers. Sutton made four All-Star teams and was elected to the Baseball Hall of Fame in 1998, his fifth year of eligibility.

❖ Red Adams

Red Adams was the Dodgers pitching coach from 1969-1980. Previous to that, Red had a long minor league playing career, winning more than 150 games in 16 seasons that straddled World War II. Red made it to the Majors for two months with the Chicago Cubs in 1946, and he lost his lone Major League decision.

A Californian by birth, Red was a Dodger scout for nearly a decade before transitioning to the coaching staff after the team moved from Brooklyn to Los Angeles.

❖ Harvey Kuenn

Harvey Kuenn (pronounced KEEN) played 15 seasons in the Majors and had a lifetime average of .303. In his rookie season in Detroit (1953), Harvey led the league with 209 hits and made the All-Star team, beginning a streak that lasted eight consecutive seasons. Harvey won the American League batting title in 1959, hitting .353 with 42 doubles. The Tigers traded him to Cleveland after that, and Harvey was with the Indians for one season before moving to the National League for the final six years of his career.

Harvey played in one World Series, his 1963 San Francisco Giants losing in seven games to the New York Yankees.

As great a hitter as Harvey Kuenn was, he is an interesting footnote in baseball pitching history for a different reason. Harvey made the final out of two of Dodger lefty Sandy Koufax's four no-hitters. In 1963, Harvey grounded back to Koufax for the final out, and two years later, Harvey struck out to end Koufax's 1965 perfect game against the Chicago Cubs.

A great baseball man, Harvey Kuenn died at home in Peoria, Arizona in 1988.

10

Ferguson Jenkins

Expanding the Strike Zone & Twin D Sends a Message

❖ Expanding the Strike Zone

In 1974, I'm with the Texas Rangers, and my catcher, Jim Sundberg, is a rookie. We're playing the Tigers, a team I had good luck against by keeping the ball down and away with a good slider.

Tiger outfielder Al Kaline, a future Hall of Famer, is an exception. I can never seem to get him out.

The game progresses to the sixth inning, and the umpire hasn't been giving me the slider down and away (from a right-handed hitter). Two sliders and Kaline checks his swing both times. Ball one. Ball two.

Behind in the count 2-0, I call time out and wave the glove for Sundberg to come out to the mound.

"Come on out," I call. "I want to talk to you."

Because the American League has the DH (designated hitter), a pitcher can't talk to the home plate umpire to plead his case because he never gets to bat. Because of that, I have to improvise.

Sunny (Sundberg) comes out to the mound.

"Just stand right here," I say. "I want to talk to the umpire. Just stand here, don't move."

The home plate umpire is getting restless and calls out to Sunny and me to quit talking and get moving.

I call back, "Hey, Ray! I need to talk to you, Ray. C'mon out here."

35

He walks out to join us. As he nears he says, "My name's not Ray."

"Yes, it is; it's Ray Charles. It'll be Stevie Wonder if you want it to be."

"Call me what you want," he laughs, "I'm Dick Stello."

The three of us are standing on the mound laughing: Stello, Sunny, and me.

At the end of the inning, I go back to the dugout and Billy Martin, our manager, wants to know what was so funny out there. So I tell him.

"Hey. I had a case to plead, so I got my point across. The only way I could do it was by telling a joke."

Not long after, Stello starts giving me that slider, down and away.

* * *

❖ Twin D Sends a Message

In 1967, I was pitching for the Cubs and squared off against Don Drysdale at Chavez Ravine (Dodger Stadium).

Drysdale guns us down in the top of the first: one, two, three, side retired.

My turn. The Dodger leadoff hitter is speedster Maury Wills. He's been stealing a lot of bases, so I work hard to keep him honest, making him skip rope (move his feet).

Wills doesn't like it. He steps back in the box and stares out at me. I throw hard inside again. Wills glares again. He fouls off a couple of pitches, but eventually I walk him.

Wills is a pretty good base runner, so I throw over to first base several times, but he gets back safely.

I look in for the sign, pause, and throw over again. Five times I throw over. The home crowd starts booing.

I deal to the plate, my first pitch to Jim Gilliam a slider that hits him on the knee. Now I have two fast runners on first and second with nobody out.

Randy Hundley (my catcher) calls time and comes out to the mound. He lifts his mask and asks, "What do you want to do?"

I said, "Sheesh, now we get Tommy Davis [two-time batting champion]. Let's see if we can get a groundball or something. We'll just work the count, hold them close so Wills won't steal third."

I throw hard in, Davis checks his swing, and I get a called strike. Hundley wants a slider. Davis grounds to (Don) Kessinger at short for a 6-4-3 double play.

With two out and Wills on third, next up is Willie Davis. He pops out on the first pitch.

I hit a guy, walk a guy, throw fourteen pitches, and get out of the inning.

Drysdale goes back out and sits my guys down one, two, three again.

My turn. At some point during the home half of the second, I probably pushed someone else off the plate.

The game progresses to the third inning, and now it's my turn to hit.

I'm walking around Dodger catcher Johnny Roseboro to the batter's box, and Roseboro says, "Be alive, young man."

I answer, "I am alive."

Drysdale's first pitch whistles behind me. I don't know how I got out of the way.

I stand back up, dusting myself off, and Roseboro says, "Get the message, young man?"

"Yeah, I got the message."

I didn't throw at anybody the rest of the game.

* * *

❖ Ferguson Jenkins

Big, strong Hall of Fame right-hander Ferguson Jenkins was a dominant starter in the Major Leagues for 19 seasons with a career record of 284-226. He won 20 or more games six times, five in a row from 1967-71 while with the Cubs. Jenkins was a powerhouse; he threw 267 complete games and pitched 4,500 innings in his Major League career. A three-time All-Star, Jenkins won the NL Cy Young award in 1971 and finished in the top three in Cy Young voting five times. He finished his long and storied career having faced 18,400 Major League hitters and giving up less than one hit per inning.

❖ Umpire Dick Stello

On November 19, 1987, Dick Stello, a umpire in the Major Leagues for more than 20 years, was crushed to death in a freak accident near Lakeland, Florida, when two cars he was standing between were hit at a high rate of speed by a third vehicle.

Stello, 53, of Pinellas Park, and Benjamin Suddarth, 48, of Seminole, were standing and talking between their parked automobiles when their vehicles were violently rear-ended along two-lane State Road 33 north of Lakeland. Stello was killed instantly. Suddarth was hospitalized in serious condition.

A former nightclub comic prior to becoming an umpire, Stello had a great sense of humor. From 1974 until shortly before his death in 1987, Stello was married to sexploitation film star Chesty Morgan (73FF-32-36). The couple had just recently divorced at the time of his passing.

❖ Don Drysdale

A dominating starter for 14 seasons with the Dodgers in both Brooklyn and Los Angeles, Drysdale was fearless when it came to pitching high, hard, and tight. A workhorse, Don won 209 games (losing 166) in his career with a sterling 2.95 ERA. An eight-time All-Star, Drysdale won the NL Cy Young Award in 1962, going 25-9. He finished nearly one-third of his career starts and threw 49 shutouts.

An excellent hitter, Drysdale clubbed 29 home runs during his career (seven in 1965) and drove in 113 runs.

Don went 3-3 in five World Series, the Dodgers winning three and losing two. Don Drysdale died unexpectedly of a heart attack on July 3, 1993. He was 56 years old.

11

Gary Carter

The 3-Man, Steve Rogers, and Spaceman Lee

One of the funniest things I remember from my playing days was a "3-man lift" that went bad during spring training back when I was with the Montreal Expos.

The 3-man lift is a prank veterans play on a rookie or baseball outsider, most commonly pulled in spring training. The key is to find the right guy who hasn't seen it before.

The joke consists of a mark (a victim) who's held down by two of the stronger veteran players in camp. The vets interlock their legs and arms, so the person in the middle is unable to move.

Another guy, usually the strongest guy in camp—or sometimes a small middle infielder chosen for dramatic effect—buckles into a weightlifting belt, stretches, flexes, and does everything he can to play up his impending fete of strength. He will lift all three players, the two side musclemen and the mark, by hoisting up the middle player solely by his belt.

As the lifter struts forward and readies for his dramatic lift, the other players on the team come from behind and douse the trapped victim with buckets of anything they can find. I had a long career and saw a lot of ingredients: tobacco juice, shaving cream, milk, and grass clippings are among my favorites.

We're doing the lift, and I am one of the two guys flanking the rookie, helping to pin him in place. We've got him good; interlocked by legs and arms, the rook is frozen in place.

Elias Sosa, a veteran relief pitcher for a number of teams, was with the Expos at the time. When Elias and the guys rush up and blast the mark with the mixture, Elias buries me too. I get drilled. Splattered like the mark.

I'm ticked off and yell at him.

"Sos, you idiot! What's the deal with you? You're only supposed to get the guy in the middle!"

Sosa shrugs. "I thought we were supposed to get all three guys."

* * *

❖ Gary on Steve Rogers

At the beginning of my career, when I was first starting out with Montreal, we had a pitcher who would shake me off all the time. No matter what I wanted to mix in, he didn't want to throw it. Pro ball is hard enough when the pitcher and catcher are in synch. When they're not—and we weren't— silent arguments between batterymates make for a long and frustrating ballgame.

I put up with it for a while but finally reached a point where I knew I needed either to smarten up or think up a way to remedy the situation.

I started firing down (calling for) fastballs on every pitch. The hitters caught on quickly, and all of a sudden, my pitcher started getting knocked around. Big League hitters can rope a fastball, especially when they know one's coming.

The pitcher finally calls time out and waves me out to the mound.

He says, "I think we have a problem here."

I reply, "You're damn right we have a problem. You keep frickin' shaking me off! Until you start believing in me, we're gonna have a problem."

We never did have a problem after that. In fact, once we got on the same page, we won a lot of games together.

Who was the pitcher? My longtime batterymate, Steve Rogers.

* * *

❖ Gary on Spaceman Lee

I played with Bill (Spaceman) Lee when Space was in his rebellious phase. Then again, those of us who knew him, played with him, or followed him throughout his career might have a tough time figuring out when he wasn't in his rebellious phase.

A lot of left-handed pitchers are off-center, but Space was one of a kind. No one else came close.

He pitched for two teams in his career, the Red Sox and the Expos. He was my teammate on the Expos, so I got to catch him. Back then, Lee has a real long beard, which manager Dick Williams shrugs off to Bill being Bill.

We are leaving on a road trip and supposed to dress professionally: nice slacks, a dress shirt, and sport coat. We could also wear designer jeans. Dress shoes were a given.

Space shows up wearing a pair of Roman sandals—which showcased the godawfulest looking feet I've ever seen—and instead of dress slacks, he's wearing khakis he cut (or tore) into shorts. He skipped the sport coat and dress shirt, too. In their place he wore an "I love Bernie Carbo" T-shirt. A backpack is slung over his shoulder.

Dick Williams looks at Lee and says, "This is no dress code. What's the deal? Where's your suitcase?"

Spaceman points to his shoulder. "Right here," he says, "my backpack."

That's the kind of guy Bill Lee was. He was a free spirit. Flaky, too. And he was a good pitcher. He won 16 ballgames the first year he came to us.

* * *

❖ Gary Carter

Hall of Fame catcher Gary Carter spent 19 seasons in the Major Leagues and was an 11-time All-Star and 3-time Gold Glove winner. He was voted into Cooperstown in 2003, his sixth year of eligibility. He won the World Series in 1986 with the New York Mets, delivering eight hits and driving in nine runs as the Mets, who won 108 games during the regular season, rallied back from the brink of defeat to beat the Boston Red Sox in seven games.

Gary hit 324 homers during his career and drove in 1,224 runs, leading the National League in 1984. He won five Silver Slugger awards, a trophy given annually to the best offensive player at each position in both the American League and the National League, as determined by the coaches and managers of Major League Baseball.

Gary Carter lives in South Florida where he coaches college baseball and is actively involved in youth-oriented charity work.

❖ Elias Sosa

Signed by the San Francisco Giants from the Dominican Republic, Sosa pitched in for eight Major League teams in his 12-year career. Almost exclusively a reliever, Elias made 601 career appearances with only three starts.

During his rookie season with the Giants, Elias won 10 games, saved 18, and pitched in 71 games.

Although he gave up just 64 homers in his 918 innings, one home run he did give up became quite famous: Sosa surrendered the second of three hit by Reggie Jackson of the New York Yankees during game six of the 1977 World Series.

In 1977 with the Dodgers and 1979 with the Montreal Expos, Elias posted earned run averages of 1.98 and 1.96. He finished his career with a 59-51 record and 83 saves.

❖ Steve Rogers

Right-hander Steve Rogers went on to win 158 games during 13 seasons with the Montreal Expos. A five-time All-Star, Rogers finished in the top three in Cy Young balloting three times and was the league ERA leader in 1982. He won 10 games as rookie and was second behind Giants outfield Gary Matthews in the voting for National League Rookie of the Year.

Rogers was a quality starter; he finished nearly one-third (129 of 393) of his Major League starts and threw 37 shutouts. He averaged less than one hit per inning and gave up only 151 home runs in 2,837 innings of work.

Once their rules of engagement were squared away, Steve Rogers and Gary Carter went on to become a terrific tandem. Rogers won 131 games and threw 110 complete games during the 10 years he and Carter were batterymates.

Since retiring, Steve Rogers has remained active in baseball circles and is currently an executive for the Major League Baseball Players Association.

❖ Bill Lee

Left-hander Bill "Spaceman" Lee pitched 14 seasons in the Major Leagues, the first 10 for the Boston Red Sox and the last four for Montreal. For all his uniqueness off the field, he was a winner. Space went 119-90 over his career, winning 17 for three straight seasons with Boston. The first of those seasons (1973) he was named to the American League All-Star team. He pitched very well in two starts during the 1975 World Series, which Boston lost to the Cincinnati Reds.

Rather than rely on just a fastball, Lee changed speeds often and threw a variation of the high-arcing, lobbed Eephus pitch called the Leephus pitch (or "Space Ball"). One of them Tony Perez hit over the Green Monster in Fenway Park for a two-run homer during game seven of the World

Series, cutting Boston's 3-0 lead to 3-2. The Reds rallied to win it, and the Series, 4-3.

One of baseball's most controversial figures throughout the decade of the 1970s, Lee has authored four books, two written with Richard Lally and two with Jim Prime. He lives in Northern California.

12

Bob Boone

Where's Pete?

Ninth inning, game six of the 1980 World Series. I'm catching for the Phillies, we're playing the Kansas City Royals, and Frank White is the hitter. White hits a foul pop toward the first base dugout.

It's a long run, but I start chasing it.

Catchers are taught that anything 45-degrees back is yours. Anything outside of that angle, keep chasing but expect the first or third baseman to make the play. Up it goes and off you go, hustling in pursuit. Wait to be called off and defer.

Wherever a foul pop is lifted, all catchers are taught to chase until being called off, especially if the ball carries outside of your geometric coverage area. As soon as Mike Schmidt or Pete Rose would say something on a foul toward third or first, I would veer off. As soon as they holler, I'm out of the play.

White's popup is toward the first base line but drifting toward the near end of our Phillies dugout. It's out of my zone, but I keep running after it, waiting to be called off.

Every step I'm thinking, "I'm waiting, I'm waiting. Where's the help?"

I continue the chase, desperately running toward the dugout. The ball's tumbling down, and I know I'm close to the steps. If I keep chasing, I'm going to fall in.

But I have to keep chasing; I'm not hearing Pete (Rose), and I'm wondering, "Where is this sonofabitch?"

I'm by the dugout, the ball's coming down, and I have no other choice—I have to lunge for it.

I expect to collide with and rebound off him (Rose). As I grab this ball, I just know he's going to hit me. Both of us will fly into the dugout.

Still I don't hear him.

I go for the ball, reaching above my head to grab it. I don't try to wait and catch it two-handed like I normally do. I tried to snatch the ball quick and hang on tight, because I know Pete's going to slam into me.

Well, after all that, the ball pops out of my glove.

Dammit! I dropped it!

The ball caroms up and out of my glove. It falls toward the ground. Suddenly, there's Pete. He's just now arriving and opportunistically grabs it. He makes the out, a crucial play in the game and the World Series.

When that baseball popped out of my glove, I wanted to kill Pete. When he caught it, I wanted to kiss him.

The moral of the story on that famous play is this: Charlie Hustle, my butt. I'm the one who hustled. Pete showed up for the rebound.

But all's well that ends well, at least in baseball. This was a key play in an historic game on baseball's greatest stage.

We won that game, and with it the World Series, Philadelphia's first. It was a big moment for the city and all the fans. The Phils were founded in 1883 and are America's oldest continuous, one-name, one-city sports team.

Despite all the Hall of Famers and All-Stars who played in that World Series, it was a hustle play on a foul ball that helped decide it.

I'm proud of that.

❖ Bob Boone

If you were to pick the least likely catcher of Bob's era to have a popup get away, he'd be at the top of your defensive list. Boone was a 7-time Gold Glover and 4-time All-Star who represented both leagues during his long and distinguished 19-year career.

A durable everyday player, Boone broke in with the Phillies in 1972. He played with the team for a decade before moving to the California Angels for seven seasons and the Kansas City Royals for two.

Boone was lifetime .254 hitter but a clutch performer, averaging .311 during eight postseason series. He was at his best during that 1980 World Series, batting .412 while driving in four runs and reaching base 11 times in 22 plate appearances. The Phillies closed out the Kansas City Royals in six games and brought the first-ever championship to their long-suffering fans.

Bob is currently a front office executive with the Washington Nationals and owns an Astroturf company with sons Bret and Matt.

❖ Pete Rose

Pete played 19 seasons for the Reds and five more with the Phillies. He played in six World Series. In this 1980 Series against Kansas City, Pete was 6-for-26 with five singles and a double.

Pete was 39 at the time, played first base every day during the regular season, and made only five errors in 1,555 chances. He made his 14th of 17 All-Star teams that summer and led the league with 42 doubles.

Never shy about taking one for the team, Pete also led the NL that season by being hit six times by pitches. During his career, he would be hit 107 times, one more than Barry Bonds. Hall of Famer Hughie Jennings got plunked the most (287), with Craig Biggio second at 285. Biggio led the National League five times, including a whopping 34—more than once a week—in 1997.

13

Gary (Sarge) Matthews and Mark Gubicza

Hotfeet

❖ Gary Matthews on Rick Sutcliffe

The Chicago Cubs made us do away with the hot foot, and for that we could credit Rick Sutcliffe. Sut and Ryne Sandberg were notorious for lighting up shoestrings of the unwary. Those two were masters.

The final straw came during a game. I have to give Sutcliffe credit; he got pretty innovative. He crawled along beneath the bench with rubbing alcohol. Sut figured out that with alcohol he could pour it all over someone's foot and then dribble a steady line away from the person. Then he could light it from a distance and take off.

Sut did, and it worked perfectly. Too perfectly. Sut actually lit someone's foot up. The whole thing—shoe, sock, pant cuff—up in flames. Sutcliffe had a future in chemistry if baseball didn't work out.

I remember this incident distinctly because we had to sit through a team meeting called specifically to announce that there would be no more hotfoots.

I forget which one of us got lit up, but when Sut lit that alcohol stream, it sounded like he lit the gas in a fireplace.

WHOOM! The player's entire foot and ankle went up in flames as he sat on the bench watching the game.

* * *

49

❖ Mark Gubicza: The Greatest Hotfoot of All-Time

While with the Royals, three of us, all pitchers—Jeff Montgomery, Bret Saberhagen, and me—found ourselves in a perfect situation. Time and teamwork took care of the rest.

Monty, Sabes, and I collected a bunch of matches and stood them around a lit cigarette. To hold everything in place, we stretched and wrapped around it a large wad of well-chewed gum.

When we finished, we knew we had something special. All we needed now was a well deserving home. Scanning around the dugout for a suitable victim, we spied first base coach Ed Napoleon.

Two of us distracted Ed, which gave the third the time to stick the mess onto the heel of one of Ed's cleats. For a low-tech innovation, it worked perfectly. The gum stuck the wad to his shoe rock-solid.

When our turn came to hit, Ed went running out to his first base coaching box. As he's standing out there, the cigarette is burning its way down toward the matches.

For Monty, Sabes, and me, watching from the bench, the anticipation from watching Ed was like waiting for our own, personal fireworks show.

Sure enough, it ignites. All the match heads zoom into flames almost instantly. When it all ignites, the flames burn high enough to brush up against Ed's leg. Ed starts jumping up and down, trying to put the fire out with everyone in the stadium watching.

The three of us are side by side in the dugout, laughing our heads off. We were semi-concerned that Ed's entire pant leg might catch fire, but not to the point we stop laughing. We can't. This is a textbook hotfoot, an instant classic that is pulled off almost too perfectly.

When the half-inning ends and Ed comes back into our dugout, he is really ticked off. After he calms down, he gets a good laugh out of it.

Hotfoots don't get much better than that. This one had it all: engineering, assembly, application, the right victim, perfect timing, and full ignition. We only wish we had it on slow-motion instant replay, igniting perfectly, just after Ed has gone out onto the field and taken his position in the coaching box. There he is, talking with the umpire at first base, the opposing infielders are warming up before the start of the inning, and Boom!

Up in smoke, right at the beginning of the inning. This was a perfect prank.

❖ Gary (Sarge) Matthews

Sarge was a hard-hitting leftfielder for five ball clubs during 16 Major League seasons, respected by his peers as an excellent pro hitter. Voted the 1973 National League Rookie of the Year after batting .300 as the everyday leftfielder for the San Francisco Giants, he was later named to the 1979 NL All-Star team while with the Atlanta Braves.

A .281 lifetime hitter, Matthews led the NL in 1984 in walks (103) and on-base percentage (.410) while with the Chicago Cubs. Sarge also played in the 1983 World Series with Philadelphia and homered in game three off Oriole lefty Mike Flanagan. The Orioles went on to beat Sarge's Phillies in five games.

His son, Gary Jr., has also had a very productive Major League career.

❖ Rick Sutcliffe

Big right-handed starting pitcher Rick Sutcliffe was Rookie of the Year in 1979 with the Dodgers, won the NL Cy Young Award in 1984 after going 16-1 following a mid-year trade to the Cubs, and was a three-time All-Star. He had 11 seasons of 10 or more wins and a career record of 171-139. He also led the National League in wins and ERA.

Nicknamed "The Red Baron" in honor of his thick, red hair, Sutcliffe has long been one of baseball's colorful personalities. He is now a popular TV commentator, often seen on network television.

❖ Ed Napoleon

Edward George Napoleon is a former minor league player, manager, and Major League coach. Ed played 14 years in the minors but never made it above AA, where he hit .240. Not a big man, Ed was primarily an outfielder who also pitched a couple dozen times in relief.

Napoleon played for the St. Louis Cardinals and Pittsburgh Pirates organizations from 1956 until 1970 and then managed and coached for the Yankees, Indians, Royals, and Orioles in the minor leagues. He also coached in the Majors for the Houston Astros and New York Yankees.

❖ Jeff Montgomery

A ninth-round draft choice out of Marshall University, long-time Kansas City closer Jeff Montgomery pitched 13 of his 14 Major League seasons for the Royals en route to 304 life-time saves. A tough right-hander, Jeff had eight seasons with 24 or more saves, including a league-high 45 in 1993.

A three-time All-Star, Montgomery had a remarkable 1989 season: 7-3, a 1.38 ERA, 18 saves, and only three home runs surrendered in 92 innings of late-inning relief.

Many of his saves came in relief of his hotfoot co-conspirators.

❖ Bret Saberhagen

Sixteen seasons, a 167-117 record, three-time All Star, and two-time Cy Young Award winner, the durable right-hander twice won 20 games, including a league leading 23-6 with a 2.16 ERA for the Royals in 1989.

Bret started and won two of the Royals' four games in their 1985 World Series win over the St. Louis Cardinals. He pitched brilliantly in the Series, giving up just 1 run, 11 hits, and 1 walk (against 10 strikeouts) in 18 innings of work. He shut the Reds out in game seven at home, scattering five hits while beating John Tudor and the Cardinals 11-0. For his work, he was named the 1985 World Series Most Valuable Player.

❖ Mark Gubicza

A big (6'6") right-handed pitcher, Mark was Kansas City's second round selection in the 1981 draft out of high school in Philadelphia. He made the Big League club three seasons later and pitched for the Royals for 13 years. He went 132-136, with a career best 20-8 season in 1988. A durable starter for much of his career, over one 3-year span he started 35, 35, and 36 games, completing 26. Eight were shutouts.

Mark was a two-time All-Star. He also won game six for the Royals in the 1985 AL Championship Series against the Toronto Blue Jays, helping the team advance to the World Series and win the world championship.

14

Bruce Benedict

A Fortunate Case of Mistaken Identity

Everybody who plays in the Big Leagues for a long time wants to think he has a big impact on his team and a big impact on his city. We like to believe that everyone knows who we are.

Back when I played for the Atlanta Braves, we had a Sunday day game, so I took my family and some friends to a local establishment famous for its great brunch.

We got the red carpet treatment. The food was great, and the service unbelievable. Waiters hovered around our table. It was as good as good gets. Maybe even better.

Well, to make a long story short, we got up to leave (there were seven or eight of us) and find ourselves surrounded by a circle of wait staff. The manager thanks us profusely for coming.

"It is great to have you here at our restaurant," he said. "Please come back at any time."

I hadn't received our bill, so I ask what I owe.

The manager says, "You don't owe us anything. Thank you for coming. You do not owe us a dime."

My family and I go back two more times, and the same thing happens: Waiters all over us, great food, on the house—no charge.

We go back a fourth time. Again we eat a great meal, enjoy impeccable service, and when time comes to leave, I ask what I owe.

The manager looks at me and smiles. "You don't owe us anything," he says. "We appreciate what you do and what you do for the city."

As I'm walking out the door with my family, I turn and thank the restaurant manager one last time.

He says, "Thank you, Mr. Murphy. Come back any time. You and your family are welcome anytime."

I hasten my exit. So I'm not Dale Murphy, two-time MVP and Hall of Fame nice guy. I'm his teammate. And that's close enough, right?

❖ Bruce Benedict

Bruce "Eggs" Benedict is a former Major League Baseball catcher who played 12 seasons for the Atlanta Braves (1978-89). He was elected to two National League All-Star teams and once led National League catchers in fielding.

Statistically, Bruce's best offensive season was 1983, when he batted .298 with two home runs and 43 runs batted in. Benedict finished with a career batting average of .242, 18 home runs, and 260 runs batted in.

Since retiring as a player, Benedict has held several positions inside the New York Mets organization and managed a farm team before becoming a scout. He also serves as a NCAA Division I college basketball official.

❖ Dale Murphy

Dale Murphy is a former two-time Major League Baseball Most Valuable Player, whose achievements occurred most notably during his years with the Atlanta Braves.

Murphy won back-to-back MVP's in the National League (1982-1983), the National League's Silver Slugger Award for outstanding hitting four straight years (1982-1985), and the National League's Gold Glove award for fielding excellence five straight years (1982-1986).

Murphy is regarded by many in baseball as one of the premier players of the 1980s. He played in seven All-Star Games and twice led the National League in home runs and runs batted in. He also led the Major Leagues in home runs and runs batted in during the decade of the 1980s. Murphy is only one of two players who hit at least 300 home runs in that decade, the other being Hall of Famer Mike Schmidt.

Murphy was awarded five consecutive Gold Gloves for fielding excellence and the Roberto Clemente Award in 1988. The Clemente Award is given annually to the Major League Baseball player who "best exemplifies the game of baseball, sportsmanship, community involvement, and the individual's contribution to his team," as voted on by baseball fans and members of the media.

A spiritual role model, Murphy and his wife Nancy have eight children. He's authored three books. Many feel Murphy's untainted, fairly earned achievements are Hall of Fame worthy. With the recent election of Andre Dawson as a "clean" player whose feats were minimized by the rampant cheating of the steroid era, perhaps there's renewed hope that someday Dale Murphy will join him in Cooperstown.

One of the most popular players in the history of the Atlanta Braves franchise, Dale Murphy is rarely mistaken for Bruce Benedict.

15

Jim Abbott

No-no in the Bronx

A no-hitter is unbelievable. The momentum that a no-hitter takes—the entire game unfolding in a different way that sort of takes on a life of its own.

In my case I had pitched against the same team—the Cleveland Indians—five days earlier. And gotten shelled.

They were a good team. Cleveland was one of the better hitting teams in the league and had a lot of weapons: Lofton, Belle, Baerga, Sandy Alomar, and Thome.

They had lit me up in Cleveland, old Municipal Stadium. I struggled through two innings and go kayoed one out into the third. My line was ugly: 7 runs, 10 hits, 5 walks. That's it, one of the worst starts of my career, and I'm out. Buck (Showalter, my manager) comes and gets me.

I was so pissed. It had been a rough season. I came to New York in a trade and had pitched all right but not as well as I could have.

After Buck took me out of the game, I went up to the locker room. I threw my glove, stomped around, and threw some other things. I pulled off my jersey and changed into my running gear and left the stadium. I went running down by the old airport, hoping to run off my frustration. I returned late in the game. The Yankees had scored 10 runs; we came all the way back and won the game.

Buck calls me into his office and asks where I had gone. Leaving the stadium during a game is a no-no in professional baseball. I told him the truth: I went for a run.

He shook his head. "No," he said. "We don't go running through the streets of Cleveland."

Great. First I get shelled, and now I'm in trouble with the manager.

We flew back to New York. My next start I'm facing the exact same team, the Indians. It's five days later, but now we're back home at Yankee Stadium. I remember thinking a lot in advance of that game. How am I going to get these guys out?

What I talk about in my motivational speeches is bringing it back to trust. Know your strength. When you're in times of difficulty and struggle, you call upon what you know and follow through with conviction and belief.

That's what I wanted to do, reestablish my strengths: cut fastball thrown aggressively to the inside part of home plate and the slider, my put-away pitch. Curveball, to keep them honest. Change speeds just a little to keep them honest.

So, I took the mound with all of that as a backdrop. Kenny Lofton leads off, bouncing up to the plate, wagging his bat. My first pitch goes all the way to the backstop.

Good trust. Good trust.

I walk Lofton to start the game. Immediately, all that unease and discomfort of the past five days comes rushing in. I've seen the replay recently, when the camera pans to Buck in the dugout, and I'm sure the unease and discomfort has found him, too.

I end up getting a double play and get out of the inning. I get back to the dugout, sit down, and breathe a big sigh of relief.

I was a little wild that day, didn't have great control. I think a lot of it was that tentativeness from the last game. A little of the wildness was due to me just letting it fly and getting a feel for the game. But as the game went on, that trust started coming back.

I get through the second inning, then the third. Sitting in the dugout, (Scott) Kamieniecki on one side, Jimmy Key on the other side. Guys I always sat next to. I always sat near the trainer, too, Steve Donahue.

Little by little, the game kept going. You don't think much about it.

I remember more about between the innings than I do about the out-on-the-field innings. After the top of the fifth inning, I come back in, sit down, put my jacket on, and look up at the scoreboard. We're winning 4-0.

I'm thinking, "That's cool. That's a little better than last time."

I notice the Indians don't have any hits, and it kind of strikes me. Up until now, I really hadn't thought about it.

So I go back out there for the sixth. What I will have to say—and I'll always be appreciative of the Yankee fans—is how early the fans started to get into the no-hitter. They started clapping a little louder with every strike and boo the umpire on every ball.

I get through the sixth and go sit down. You know the old baseball no-hitter superstitions and clichés: things are a little quieter in the dugout. Drama is starting to build. Kamenicki and Key, my boys, sit a little farther away.

I remember looking up at the scoreboard after the sixth inning and thinking, "Wow, nine outs. That could happen. That's not all that unreasonable."

Then it became a battle of discipline. Bringing it back to trust. In a no-hitter, you start getting all this other stuff mixed in. Hopefulness comes in. You start hoping for results that you can't control. So I had to go back to what I learned between starts: come at them with complete conviction.

In the Indians half of the seventh inning, Wade Boggs (my third baseman) makes an unbelievable stop and gets us a double play. So I retreat to the dugout and sit there, six outs left. With each passing Indian out, I'm mentally counting down.

I work through the eighth inning, the fans erupting with every out. They are on their feet, going crazy. Yankee Stadium is alive. The infielders are zipping it around after every out. It is unbelievably exciting. In that atmosphere, the last out of the eighth inning triggers an eruption from the stands. Inning over, you run off the field to a rocking stadium, the fans all screaming and yelling. You feel their emotion, their excitement. Out by out the momentum keeps building.

You get to the dugout and sit down. You are, literally, all by yourself. Nobody around. Nobody talking to you. It's the first time in your life that you hope your team doesn't score because you want to get right back out onto the field.

We make our last out in the bottom of the eighth. I remove my jacket, walk up those steep Yankee Stadium steps, and jog onto the field. The place is going crazy. My knees are knocking. My heart is racing.

Matty Nokes is catching that day, and we have a great back and forth; he is awesome that day. I am taking my warm-up pitches, looking around, trying to calm my nerves.

Just make a pitch, with trust.

Lofton comes up to bat. Top of the order. It always seems to work that way in a game that really matters. Top the ninth, top of the order. Kenny Lofton was arguably the fastest player in the league. He lays down a bunt, in a 4-0 game. The ball trickles foul.

Bunting in the ninth inning to try and break up a no-hitter is considered taboo by baseball standards. The place goes berserk.

Yankee Stadium rains down its displeasure with deafening boos. The fans are yelling, screaming at Lofton.

Lofton steps back, gets reset, then steps back in the batter's box with a smirk on his face. I have said often that Yankee fans shamed him into swinging the bat. I'm glad they did. He hit a ground ball to second base. One out.

The next hitter is Felix Fermin. First pitch fastball, and he hits it a ton, a long fly ball to deep center field. Bernie Williams chases it down. Two outs. Bernie fires it back in, the guys toss ball around infield, and the fans are on feet. I stand there on the mound and receive the ball, now just one out away.

Carlos Baerga, a switch hitter, defies conventional baseball wisdom and turns around to hit lefty (I throw left-handed) because he doesn't like the ball inside, and that's where I'd pound my slider.

Slider, outside part of the plate. Carlos slaps a groundball to shortstop, what seems like a 30-hopper that takes forever to cross the infield. Randy Velarde comes up on it, gloves it, and throws it across the diamond to Mattingly at first. Donnie catches it for the final out. He throws his hands in the air in jubilation.

I'm there on the mound, watching. All I can think is, "Oh, yeh."

It is a very surreal moment.

Then and now, that moment reminded me a lot of the Olympics. The last out of the 1988 Olympic (exhibition) gold medal game felt much the same. Groundball to Robin (Ventura) who threw it across to Tino (Martinez). Then came the celebration.

Same thing happened in the no-hitter. Grounder to the left side, final out secured, then the celebration. The world just seems to stop. Five days before I am running through the streets of Cleveland frustrated and angry. How does this happen?

It's a wonderful lesson of sports. You get knocked down and—just by getting up, thinking about what you do best with belief and conviction—you can have an entirely different result. Things may be tough now, but you never know what might happen tomorrow.

This game was a lesson in believing in myself, and the power that belief serves to create. I think it's a lesson that applies to all of us.

❖ Jim Abbott

Abbott was born and raised in Flint, Michigan, won the Sullivan Award as the nation's best amateur athlete in 1987, and was drafted in the first round of baseball's 1988 draft. A year later, he was in the Major Leagues and pitched in the Majors for more than a decade.

Abbott won 88 games in the Majors, a sterling feat for a remarkable athlete born without a right hand. Although he pitched for most of his career in the American League, a brief stint with the Milwaukee Brewers at the end of his career allowed him to bat. Having tripled once in spring training once off veteran pitcher Rick Reuschel, Abbott had two hits in regular season play for the Brewers.

Count Yankee closer Mariana River among Jim's fans, he's still in awe from watching Abbott hit one-handed home runs during batting practice.

Jim Abbott lives in Southern California and is a widely respected motivational speaker.

16

Rob Dibble

Spring Training Prank War: Scudder vs. Charlton

Scott Scudder was a Paris, Texas boy, Norm Charlton attended Rice University in Houston, and the two were locked in a huge feud of practical jokes when Nike introduced its innovative line of air-soled, bubble running shoes.

We were teammates on the Reds and didn't get custom-made spikes, so anything new was cherished. I don't care how much money you make—whenever you get a brand new pair of sneakers, it's like Christmas.

We all took excellent care of the stuff we already had. Norm and I doted over our spikes. No one else was allowed to clean them—this was our superstition. We also insisted on hanging our own stuff in our lockers and protected our gear by taping our travel bags shut. On the tape we'd write, "Don't open." It was kind of weird, but that's the way we did things.

Randy Myers was like that, too. He shared our superstition. Do not touch my stuff. We didn't want anybody's bad luck rubbing off on our gloves, shoes, or anything else. The three of us were like Francis "Psycho" Sawyer in the movie Stripes. "Don't touch me, and don't touch my stuff."

After each game, I used a wire brush to clean my shoes. Norm and Randy did the same thing.

Scudder and Norm are immersed in their ongoing spring training prank duel when Scott takes Norm's new 180 Nikes, the ones with the bubble sole. Scudder pops the bubbles and freezes the shoes in a bucket.

Norm loves those shoes, so when they go missing, Norm goes bananas. When he finds them, the bubbles are popped, and the shoes are ruined.

Later in spring training, we have a rainout, and Scudder is busy throwing in the cages. Norm comes and finds me and asks for help finding some cinderblocks. I have no idea what he's thinking and do not ask. I just help him look.

I'm running around the complex, pulling tarps off mounds to borrow the cinderblocks that hold them down.

Since it's raining, the ground crew is ticked.

"Dibble! Where are you going with that?"

"Don't worry about it. I'll bring it back in a little bit."

Sometimes in spring training, players get car deals. The player gets to use the car for six weeks in exchange for an appearance at the dealership or being in an ad.

Well, this spring Scudder has gotten his first car deal. A Jeep dealer right down the street from our complex in Plant City bartered him a new Cherokee.

Cinderblocks in hand, Norm and I look for a car jack. The plan is to remove all four wheels off Scudder's car. One of the other players has an old car, but its jack is a piece of crap. We take it. It's pouring rain, but here we go—two idiots in the parking lot, jacking up a Jeep Cherokee, taking off its tires, and blocking the axles with cinderblocks.

We finish and admire our work. Then we stack all four tires on the Cherokee's roof.

The players' parking lot was between the batting cages and clubhouse. After Scudder finishes throwing and starts for the clubhouse, he comments on a car in the parking lot to pitching coach Larry Rothschild.

Scott says, "What idiot would have all four of his tires on top of his truck?"

Then he looks closer and almost cries when he realizes the car he's talking about is his brand new loaner Cherokee.

Revenge is sweet, and that was just one of dozens of practical jokes that Norm masterminded and I helped pull off.

Some guys you could pick on, others you couldn't. Norm Charlton was at the top of the couldn't list. He was a master.

❖ Rob Dibble

Big, powerful right-handed flame thrower Rob Dibble's career was short but exciting. A two-time All-Star in seven seasons, Dibble did not present much mystery to hitters. He was going to throw you a fastball. Your challenge was to hit it.

More failed than succeeded. In 1992, Dibble averaged 14.1 strikeouts per nine innings pitched. He averaged 12.2 Ks per nine innings for his career. In 477 innings of work, he gave up 332 hits and struck out 645—nearly twice as many.

Dibble was Cincinnati's first round pick in 1983 out of Florida Southern College. He spent six years working his way through the minors before reaching the Big Leagues mid-season in 1988.

He helped Cincinnati win the 1990 World Series over Oakland, winning game two in relief. Hall of Famer Dennis Eckersley took the loss.

❖ Scott Scudder

Spot-starter and reliever Scott Scudder went 21-34 in five Major League seasons with the Cincinnati Reds and Cleveland Indians. He was a teammate of Dibble and Charlton from 1989-91 and pitched 1 1/3 scoreless innings in the Reds' 1990 World Series win against the Oakland A's. Although eclipsed as a pitcher by the other two, Scudder retired with something Dibble and Charlton never experienced: he hit a Major League home run.

❖ Norm Charlton

Norm (The Sheriff) Charlton was Cincinnati's first round choice the year after Dibble, and the two quickly became very close friends. Originally from Louisiana, Charlton matriculated to Rice University and played for three years.

A sometimes starter his first three seasons for Cincinnati, Charlton moved to the bullpen and short relief for good in 1992. He saved 26 games that year, a career high, and was named to the National League All-Star team. Like Dibble, Charlton also pitched in relief for Cincinnati during the team's 1990 World Series win over Oakland.

He would pitch during three more postseasons while with Seattle, but Norm never again returned to the Series. He was nails in October, posting a microscopic 1.08 ERA in 17 appearances in postseason play.

17

Mark Grace

Sutcliffe and the Straightjacket

When we played together on the Cubs, Rick Sutcliffe was my best friend on the team. He's got a good sense of humor. To this day Sut still calls me "Kid."

One day he just starts burying me. I'm a rookie, so I take it for a while but not forever. I wave him away with, "Aww, c'mon. Leave me alone, old man." Or something to that effect.

Two days go by. Not a word is said between us. Nothing. Not even a grunt. The third day I amble into the clubhouse and freeze when I see what's waiting: three very large and powerful humans waiting with a straightjacket. In less than a minute, Rick Sutcliffe, Goose Gossage, and Jody Davis are stuffing me into it. One grabs me by the feet, one's got me around the waist, and the third has me hammerlocked by the neck.

Once I'm buckled up—helplessly hog-tied—they drag me into the trainer's room and slam me face-first onto the trainer's table. I'm pinned down.

Out of the corner of my eye, I can see what's coming next—a freaking mountain of trainer's tape.

The three of them disappear into blurs and windmills of tape. In a matter of minutes, I am securely taped to the trainer's table. The more I struggle, the more tape I get. They have me wrapped down so tightly, I can't move. I am mummified on top of the trainer's table.

Sut then turns to John Fierro, our trainer, and says, "If you untape him, you're going on the table next."

The trainer nods. Then he bends over near my ear and says, "Gracie, I can't undo you, dude."

With that, the three gorillas leave the room and head out for batting practice. Not long after those three go out to loosen up, my group is due to hit. Our manager, Don Zimmer, calls out, "Anybody seen Grace? Where the f*$#%! is Grace?"

Sut shrugs and says, "I don't know."

"I don't know, either," adds Gossage.

"Not a clue," calls out Jody Davis.

Finally, John Fierro sidles over next to Zim and says matter-of-factly, "Gracie's taped to the trainer's table."

I am on that table a good 45 minutes, pinned and helpless, unable to move. I'll die there if someone doesn't free me. That whole time the other three are outside hitting and shagging balls, I'm in the clubhouse yelling, "HEYYYY . . . ANYBODY! HELLLP!! UNDO ME!!!"

I could have hollered forever. There is nobody in there but the clubhouse kids, and they have gotten the same threat: if you undo him, you're next.

So, finally, Zimmer comes into the trainer's room, sees me, and just starts laughing. He says, "What the f*$#%! did you do to deserve this?"

"I called Sut an old man."

I know that's what I'm being punished for because Sut and the others kept chanting my crime while taping me.

"Who's an old man now? This old man is taping you to the trainer's table."

So, looking back, I got about 45 minutes of trainer's table time and learned a very valuable lesson. If you're 24 and a guy much bigger than you is 32, never say a word.

❖ Mark Grace

A three-time All-Star and four-time Gold Glove winner at first base, Mark finished runner-up that season for NL

Rookie of the Year, an award won by Chris Sabo of the Cincinnati Reds. Grace was a terrific left-handed hitter, batting .300 or better nine times and .303 for his career.

A durable player and disciplined hitter, Grace averaged 140 games and 152 hits for each of his 16 seasons. He finished with 2,445 hits and 511 doubles, 51 when he led the league in 1995. He walked nearly twice as often as he struck out and finished with a .383 on-base percentage.

In Mark's 15th season, he reached the World Series with the Arizona Diamondbacks and reached base nine times in six games as Arizona beat the New York Yankees in six games. He also pitched an inning that season, giving up Dodger catcher David Ross' first career home run during a 19-1 blowout defeat.

Colorful and quotable, Grace lives in Arizona and is a TV commentator for the Diamondbacks.

❖ Rick Sutcliffe

During Gracie's 1988 rookie season, Sutcliffe was 32 in his tenth. Sutcliffe led the league with 18 wins the year before, one of nine seasons in which he'd record double digit victory totals.

Sutcliffe is an imposing man (6'7") and came to the Majors quickly. A first-round choice by the Dodgers in 1974 out of Van Horn High School in Kansas City, Rick was pitching in the Majors two years later at the age of 20. Although sent down for more seasoning, Rick returned ready to fire in 1979.

He was twice a post-season starter for the Cubs but neither team, in 1984 against the San Diego Padres or 1989 against the San Francisco Giants, could advance out of the National League Championship Series.

Sutcliffe could help himself with the bat, too. In 1979, he drove in 17 runs while batting .247 with three doubles and a home run in 40 games for the Dodgers. He had a big year on the hill that season too, going 17-10. He was an easy winner for National League Rookie of the Year, earning 83 percent of the vote.

Now a popular and sometimes outspoken broadcaster, Sutcliffe remains a very popular baseball personality from coast-to-coast.

18

Goose Gossage

Billy Martin &
Ron Guidry

Back in 1978, Yankee left-hander Ron Guidry was phenomenal. He went 25-3. It was a Cy Young year that remains the most amazing season I ever saw a pitcher have. His earned run average was microscopic, and he averaged less than one runner per inning, hits and walks combined. It was remarkable consistency and effectiveness, especially since he threw around 275 innings with 16 complete games and 9 shutouts.

Well, on one of his rare off nights, Guidry is in a jam (one of his few) and is clearly struggling. Billy Martin is our manager and doesn't like what he sees. Billy looks over to our pitching coach, Art Fowler.

"Goddammit, Art," he barks. "Go out there and see what the hell is going on."

Art calls time and runs out to the mound.

Gator (Guidry's nickname) looks at Art and asks, "Art, what am I doing wrong?"

Art replies, "I don't know what you're doing wrong. But whatever you're doing, quit it. It sure is pissing Billy off."

❖ Ron Guidry

Gator was a dominating left-hander for nine straight seasons with the Yankees, going 154-67 between 1977-1985. As tough as there was in baseball during his peak, Guidry also won five Gold Gloves for his fielding and made four All-Star teams. He finished his 14-year career in 1988 with a record of 170-91 and an earned run average of 3.29.

Ron was 5-2 in 10 postseason starts, 3-1 in his three World Series (all Yankee victories). He pitched 32 innings in the World Series, giving up just 20 hits. After retiring, Ron later returned to the Yankees as manager Joe Torre's pitching coach.

❖ Billy Martin

Hard-living, hard-drinking, hard as nails as a player and manager, Billy Martin was born and raised in Berkeley, California. An infielder during his playing days, Martin played half of his 11-year career for the Yankees before bouncing around through six other teams. A consistent .250 hitter, Martin was mostly a role player, known for his intense style of play on the field and late night exploits.

Billy made one All-Star team and in 1956 got to pinch-hit for the AL and manager Casey Stengel.

As mediocre as Billy's regular season stats always seemed to be, he was a money player who raised his game in the postseason. Martin hit .333 in five World Series, helping the Yankees to four wins: against the New York Giants in 1951 and the Brooklyn Dodgers in 1952, 1953, and 1956.

He was at his best in 1953, going 12-for-24 with two homers and eight runs batted in to lead the Yankees to a six-game series win.

After retiring as a player in 1961, Billy returned to the dugout in 1969 to begin an 18-year career as a manager. He was in the dugout for five different American League clubs: Minnesota, Detroit, Texas, Oakland, and the New York Yankees.

In two stints covering eight years with the Yankees, Martin managed the ballclub to two pennants and the 1977 World Series championship.

Billy died in a one-car crash on Christmas Day, 1989 in Johnson City, New York. He was 61.

19

Larry Andersen

Sloanie's Ranchero, Tekulve & Carlton, & Bedrock Takes Out the Trash

❖ Sloanie's Ranchero

Going back to my first couple years, I came up through the minor leagues with Dennis Eckersley. He was a different character. I loved him, but he was crazy. Despite that or because of it, we ended up becoming very close friends.

I was drafted in 1971, and I think Eck was two years later. Our number one pick the year I came out was a guy named Dave Sloan. Sloan was from Santa Clara. The three of us hung together a fair amount. Since Eck was from Fremont (California) and Sloanie was from Santa Clara, whenever we played in Reno, we would take trips to Sloanie's place or Eck's.

Sloan drove a Ranchero, a car-sized truck with a flatbed. Different from the El Camino, the Ranchero had ridges that ran the length of the truck bed.

It was the end of August, and the minor league season lasted until the fourth of September. None of us was making much money at the time; I'm clearing $202 every two weeks. Eck was a third round pick, Sloanie was number one, and I was a seventh-rounder, so I was probably hurting the worst.

Well, none of us wanted to pay rent for the final four days of the season. We would have had to pay for the entire month had we stayed in the apartment for even just four days.

For the last three nights of our season, all three of us slept in the back bed of Sloanie's Ranchero. We tried sleeping

73

bags, blankets, anything and everything—but still woke up each morning sore from our feet to our foreheads, those stupid truck-bed ridges running the length of our bodies.

We had no other option. With the three of us wedged in there, we had no room to move.

Stories like this are what I remember most: survival, adaptation, and male bonding. It's what baseball's really all about, isn't it?

* * *

❖ Tekulve & Carlton

We were all on the Phillies in spring training at Clearwater in 1986. Kent Tekulve has a nice plan: He rents a room at the Sheraton Santee, plus a projector and big-screen to watch the NCAA basketball tournament's Final Four and, two days later, the national championship game.

Tekulve does it right. He orders in food—hors d'oeuvres—and basically sets us up with an open bar.

By the time the second half of the championship game rolls around, no one can see the action. The game is being projected onto roast beef.

The screen he rented is totally covered in cold cuts, mayo, mustard, and potato salad. What starts as a college basketball telecast has denigrated into an Animal House food fight.

After our final soldier falls from fatigue and the food war finally reaches a cease-fire, Teke surveys the damage. The bigger the mess, the more expensive the problem.

"This is going to cost me five or six grand," he says. "I'll have to pay for everything that's messed up."

I remember Lefty (Steve Carlton) repeating that the next day and adding—and I'll paraphrase it— "Teke, you f*$#%! up. You trusted us."

From that point on, off the field life was pretty chaotic. The team adopted the Flintstones TV show theme song but called ourselves the Animals and wrote A's on our hats with

Sharpie markers. Throughout spring training, we'd pile on a bus for a game somewhere and just start singing (to the Flintstones melody), "When you're with the Animals, have a yabba-dabba-do time . . ."

The whole bus would be singing.

Breaking spring camp, we flew to Cincinnati to open the season, and the Animals kept after it. On regular season trips, we'd bring beer on the bus, and Lefty would decide when it was time for everyone to start doing cannonballs.

We had everyone on the bus popping down beers and smashing the empty cans against his forehead. Nobody was excluded. One trip we pile off the bus, and Lefty's forehead is all cut up from smashing beer cans.

We were a close-knit bunch. Credit Tekulve for that.

* * *

❖ Bedrock Takes Out the Trash

After I retired, several former ballplayers were down in Florida to help put on a dream week baseball fantasy camp. Bedrock (Steve Bedrosian) was down there with me. He and I were managers. Shortly after we got there, one of the fantasy campers made fun of Bedrock's shirt. Said it looked like a picnic tablecloth.

Bedrock played this up for five days. He refused to talk to this guy, and if they passed in the clubhouse, Bedrock just glared at him. For good measure, he'd add a loud expletive.

Somehow or other Bedrock got hold of a photo of the fantasy camper posed in his batting stance. The shot was from the shoulders up, showing the fellow wearing a batting helmet and holding a bat.

Bedrock draws a bulls-eye on the camper's neck and hangs the doctored photo in the guy's locker. The next day several other campers are hovering around that locker, pointing to the photo, and blaming the threat on Bedrock. Agitators, they were.

Bedrock sees the crowd and walks over. He tells the guy, "When you come up, even if I'm not supposed to pitch against your team, I'm going to pitch against you." Having dead-faced this guy all week, he threatens him and walks away.

Game time rolls around, and the camper's spot in the batting order finally comes up. Everyone is looking for Bedrock. Someone finds him in the clubhouse, and he comes running out just to pitch to this guy.

But as Bedrock arrives, the camper's nowhere to be found. He's disappeared. People are wondering if the guy got scared and skipped town.

All of a sudden, two of the guy's teammates come around the dugout struggling to carry a big garbage can, the kind with a fold-over lid.

With one guy on each side of the garbage can, they slowly shuffle it toward the plate. A baseball bat sticks out from beneath the lid.

The guy Bedrock planned to drill is hiding inside the garbage can.

The camper's teammates set the garbage can at home plate. The lid cracks open a little bit wider, and the bat slides out a little farther, taking practice swings out over the plate.

Bedrock looks in and scratches his head. He's about to face a guy in a trash can in the batter's box, the bat moving back and forth from beneath the lid of the garbage can.

At this point of his post-Big League career, Bedrock was still able to throw, I'm guessing, the mid-to-upper eighties.

Bedrock yells in, "You ready?"

The camper wiggles his bat. Bedrock winds up and throws a fastball that slams into the middle of the garbage can. We hear a loud thud and reactive grunt, like a blend of "Wham!" and "Ugh!"

The guy felt it. Bedrock didn't hurt the guy but smoked him pretty good.

Not a lot of guys off the street can take a Major League heater in the side. But if you decide to give it a try and see what it's like, it'll hurt a lot less in a big, comfy trashcan.

* * *

❖ Dave Sloan

Dave was selected 9th overall by the Indians in the first round of the 1971 amateur draft. Nineteen of the 24 players selected made it to the Major Leagues, including Hall of Famer Jim Rice. Rice was taken 15th by Boston.

Pitchers Frank Tanana and Rick Rhoden were among that year's class who made it, Tanana taken 13th by the California Angels with Rhoden going 20th to the Dodgers. Tanana won 240 games in his career, Rhoden 151. The pair combined to make five All-Star teams.

Sloan never made it the Major Leagues. Beset with arm troubles, he pitched five seasons in the low to mid-minors, never advancing past AA. He retired in 1976 at the age of 24.

❖ Dennis Eckersley

A starter the first half of his career and a shut-down closer the second half, Dennis Eckersley's remarkable career included winning both the Cy Young Award and the league's Most Valuable Player in 1992. Eck went 7-1 with a 1.91 ERA and saved 51 games that season for the Oakland A's.

Eckersley's record was 197-171 and he saved 390 games. He was named to six All-Star teams, the first coming at age 22 and the last at 37. Dennis pitched in seven postseason seasons and saved the final game of Oakland's World Series sweep over the San Francisco Giants in the 1989 earthquake series.

Eckersley was voted into the Baseball Hall of Fame in 2004, his first year of eligibility.

❖ Kent Tekulve

One of baseball's toughest closers, tall, lanky, submarining, and bespectacled right-hander Kent Tekulve was a late inning specialist for 16 seasons. He finished his career 94-90 with a sterling lifetime ERA of 2.85. Twelve of his losses came despite giving up zero earned runs.

Tekulve was an ironman; he appeared in 1,050 games—all in relief—and saved 184. He was also very difficult to hit, posting a lifetime .244 collective average for the 6,000 men who stepped in against him. Only 63 ever touched him for a home run, barely one per every hundred hitters.

Tekulve spent his entire career in the National League, his first eleven seasons with the Pittsburgh Pirates. Three times he appeared in 90 or more games, which only two men have done—Tekulve and Mike Marshall. The third time he did that, Kent was 40 years old.

Tekulve was instrumental in the Pirates' 1979 comeback during the "We Are Family" World Series win against the Baltimore Orioles. He pitched in five of the seven games and saved three of them. Twice a top five finisher in the Cy Young voting, Kent represented Pittsburgh in the 1980 All-Star game.

❖ Steve Carlton

One of baseball's greatest left-handed pitchers, Hall of Famer Steve Carlton dominated hitters for 24 years. Lefty's career record was 329-244; he won 10 or more games 18 years in a row. He struck out 4,136 batters, completed 254 starts, and threw 55 shutouts.

Six times a 20-game winner, Carlton made 10 All-Star teams. He won four Cy Young awards as the National League's best pitcher, all with the Philadelphia Phillies: 1972, 1977, 1980, and 1982.

Carlton pitched his first seven seasons with the St. Louis Cardinals before being traded to Philadelphia straight up for

Rick Wise. Lefty spent 15 years with the Phillies before being released mid-season 1986. He also pitched briefly for San Francisco, Cleveland, the Chicago White Sox, and retired with Minnesota in 1988 at age 43.

A very good hitting pitcher, Carlton socked 13 career homers and drove in 140 runs. He was a lifetime .201 hitter. He was elected easily to the Hall of Fame his first year of eligibility. Also going in that year were longtime NL manager Leo Durocher and former Yankee shortstop Phil Rizzuto.

❖ Steve Bedrosian

The 1987 NL Cy Young Award winner with 40 saves in 56 appearances for the Philadelphia Phillies, Bedrock pitched for 14 years. He appeared in 732 games and had a lifetime record of 76-79 with 184 saves and a 3.38 ERA. He and Larry Andersen were teammates in Philadelphia for the first six weeks of the 1986 season before Andersen was released; Larry signed three days later with the Houston Astros and helped the team reach the NLCS.

20

Will Clark

Old Goat & Pack Mule

When infielder Mark McLemore and I played together on the Texas Rangers, he used to call me "Old Goat" and I used to call him "Old Pack Mule." Mark and I were the two oldest players on the team.

I'm usually one of the first to arrive in the clubhouse before a game but often the last to come back in after batting practice. In that regard, this day was no different. When I come back to the clubhouse and see everyone looking at me, I know instantly that something is wrong.

Tied to my locker, standing peacefully and wearing a (Will) Clark #22 jersey, is a goat. Nearby is a steaming mound of goat poop.

I walk closer and notice the goat is chewing something—one of my fielder's gloves. He has already eaten a pair of my spikes.

Everyone gets a real good chuckle out of that one. They also watch to see how I'll react, whether I'll be upset. I take it in stride. It's a good prank, and I have a good laugh about it.

I let a couple weeks go by so things would quiet down and guys would forget about the goat. I make a couple phone calls to some Texas farmers I know, and they are glad to help me out.

One day I bring a mule into the clubhouse. I dress him smartly in a McLemore jersey and station him in front of Mark's locker.

The moral of the story is simple: Mules poop more than goats.

❖ Will Clark

Born and raised in New Orleans, Will (The Thrill) Clark was a fourth round draft choice by Kansas City out of high school but went to Mississippi State instead of turning pro. He was richly rewarded. Will was the second pick in the 1985 draft, selected by the San Francisco Giants immediately after the Milwaukee Brewers took University of North Carolina shortstop B. J. Surhoff. Following Clark in that year's famous draft were pitcher Bobby Witt, shortstop Barry Larkin, a miss named Kurt Brown, and an Arizona State outfielder named Barry Bonds.

A six-time All-Star, in 1991 Will won one of his two Silver Sluggers as well as a Gold Glove. Known for his sweet left-handed swing, Clark retired after 15 seasons with a lifetime average of .303. Twelve times he batted .300 or better and in 1988 led the National League in runs batted in (109) and walks (100).

Will batted .333 in seven postseason series spanning 31 games. He played in one World Series, the Giants' 1989 loss to the cross-town rival Oakland A's during what later became known as "the Earthquake Series." Clark was instrumental in helping the Giants reach the Series. He was MVP in the NLCS, going 13-for-20 with eight RBIs in San Francisco's 5-game series victory over the Chicago Cubs.

Hampered by injuries his final few seasons, Will the Thrill hung up his cleats at the age of 36 to return to Louisiana. But he was swinging 'til the end. Will Clark's final season, split between Baltimore in the American League and St. Louis in the National, he hit 21 homers and batted .319.

❖ Mark McLemore

Veteran infielder Mark McLemore spent 19 seasons in Major League baseball, breaking in with the California Angels at the age of 21. He played for seven teams and spent five seasons with both Texas and California. A .259 lifetime hitter with good speed, Mark stole 272 bases and scored 943 runs during his career. A good fielder and unselfish team player, six times Mark was in the top ten in sacrifices during a season.

Mark made it to the postseason five times but never got to the World Series, losing the League Championship Series twice to the Yankees (2000-01) while with the Seattle Mariners.

Will Clark and Mark McLemore were teammates on the Rangers for four years, from 1995-98. When teasing each other about being the Old Goat and Old Pack Mule, Clark was 34 and McLemore was 33.

21

Jim Fregosi

My Wife, Your Ball

Midway through the 1978 season, I went from being a bench player for the Pittsburgh Pirates one day to manager of the California Angels the next.

It's mid-June, and my first day on the job I stress to my new ballclub that I do not care for team meetings. So what happens? I'm forced to start Day Two with a team meeting, baseball in-hand.

"Gentlemen," I begin, looking around the room at my players, "I do not like these things (meetings), but when I gave you the rules yesterday I obviously forgot one: nobody sleeps with the manager's wife except the manager."

I toss the baseball to infielder Bobby Grich, who was a bachelor. Grich had signed the ball yesterday, adding mention of an establishment he planned to visit after the game. Then he had the ball delivered to an attractive woman he'd spotted in the crowd.

That woman was my wife.

❖ Jim Fregosi

Six-time All-Star Jim Fregosi played 18 seasons in the Major Leagues, most prominently with the Angels. A .265 hitter, Fregosi hit 151 home runs and drove in 706. He also hit 78 triples and led the American League with 13 in 1968, the "Year of the Pitcher." He was the AL Gold Glove winner at shortstop in 1967 and hit .290 that season, his career high.

Jim retired as a player in mid-1978 and took over from Dave Garcia as Angels manager. He managed for 15 seasons in the Majors and won the NL pennant with the Philadelphia Phillies in 1993. After beating the Atlanta Braves to reach the World Series, Jim's Phillies lost in six games to the Toronto Blue Jays.

❖ Bobby Grich

Second baseman Bobby Grich played seven seasons with the Orioles and 10 with the California Angels, four with Fregosi as his manager. A six-time All Star, Grich won four Gold Gloves and one Silver Slugger. He tied for the league lead in home runs in strike-shortened 1981 with 22 in 100 games, and led the league outright in slugging percentage at .543. A tough and gritty player, Grich also led the league when he was hit by a pitch 20 times during the 1973 season with the Orioles.

Bobby played in the ALCS five times but never made it to the World Series.

Author's note: This story was supplied to Gregg in person by Jim Fregosi. An earlier version appeared in Playboy Magazine, as told to Tracy Ringolsby.

22

Jamie Quirk

Where's George?

When you play on a team with a hitter as great as George Brett, you never think he will ever go in a slump. Guys like George simply don't have slumps. Slumps are for regular guys like me and the rest of the fellows—certainly not for a Hall of Famer who almost hit .400.

The slumps George did have were obviously a little different from mine and everyone else's. While the rest of us mortals were grinding through a 2-for-30 stretch, a slump for George might be 2-for-12. That was about as deep as it got and as long as it lasted.

We are playing at home in Kansas City one day, and George is in one of his slumps. He makes an out and goes straight back to the dugout and then keeps going, disappearing into the tunnel. We hear him in there, rattling things around, tearing things up. George would do that every now and then, so no one paid any attention.

After that inning's third out, we retake the field. I hustle back out to catch the top half of the inning. We finish up with the pitcher's warm-ups and are nearly ready to resume play.

But the infield can't complete the ritual of throwing the ball around the horn: we have no third baseman.

The home plate ump looks at me and asks, "Where's George?"

All I can do is shrug and say, "I have no idea."

Guys start looking for him. He isn't in the dugout, so they go and check the tunnel. A huge trashcan stands against the tunnel wall, one of those oversized ones with the hinged plastic lid that lifts to open or close.

On a hunch, one of the guys opens the lid and peeks in.

"Found him," he calls out.

There George sits, inside the trash can, brooding and stewing in the darkness with the lid closed.

Once found he sticks his head out and says, "I f@#$% quit! That's it, I quit! I can't hit anymore."

So there we are, waiting out on the diamond to throw the ball around the infield and get back to playing the game, and what have we got? Our All-Star third baseman, a future first ballot Hall of Famer, holed up in a trashcan.

The game is delayed up for just a minute or two, but it certainly seems longer. It takes a little coaxing, but George climbs back out of the trashcan and runs back out to third base.

❖ Jamie Quirk

You know a guy's spent a lot of time in the Big Leagues when he's worn eleven different uniform numbers. Quirk, a journeyman catcher and sometimes third baseman, played 18 seasons in the Major Leagues, 11 with the Royals during three different stops in Kansas City.

Jamie played every position at least once, except for pitcher. Sound defensively, Jamie led all American League catchers in throwing out base stealers during the 1986 season, gunning down three out of every five who tried.

An all-state quarterback in high school, Jamie turned down a football scholarship offer from Notre Dame in order to play baseball.

❖ George Brett

Four men in the history of baseball have 3,000 hits, 300 home runs, and a lifetime .300 average. George Brett is one. Hank Aaron, Willie Mays, and Stan Musial are the others.

A second round draft choice from El Segundo High School (just south of Los Angeles International Airport), George spent his entire Major League career—21 seasons—with the Kansas City Royals, the team that selected him.

His 3,154 lifetime hits are the most ever for a third baseman. In addition to a lifetime .305 batting average, George hit 317 home runs and drove in 1,595.

If baseball awards it, chances are good Brett got it at some point during his Hall of Fame career. A 13-time All-Star, George led the Royals to a World Series championship in 1985. He also won a Gold Glove, was a three-time Silver Slugger award winner, and was the 1980 American League MVP.

George was inducted into the Baseball Hall of Fame in 1999, his first year of eligibility. He earned 98.2% of all votes cast (488 of 497).

Brett wore number 25 during his first two Major League seasons, and then switched to number 5. He wore that number for the next 19 years; he and it made each other famous.

Brett finished his remarkable 21-season career following baseball's 1993 season. The Royals retired George's number 5 the very next year.

23

Rex Hudler

The Night Cal
Broke the Record

I have been a blessed man. I didn't realize that when I signed out of my Fresno high school in 1978 that I was going learn life's lessons through baseball.

I had plenty of time to learn these things because I had to play about 10 years in the minors. It was really tough, at times a very hard road. To be 17 and competing in pro leagues against guys out of college who are three or more years older forced me to learn a lot.

Baseball teaches humility, and I was an early learner. Little did I realize when I signed as a teenage first-rounder that it was going to take me a decade to reach the Majors. When the Yankees drafted me the 18th selection overall, I figured that by 21, I would be a Big Leaguer.

But things don't happen the way we want, and my career was slow to evolve. I got my cup of coffee in 1984 with Yogi Berra as my first manager, but (Yankee owner George) Steinbrenner fired Yogi at year's end.

Billy Martin replaced Yogi. I got to play for him briefly and see his managerial style. That off-season the Yankees traded me to the Orioles, whose manager was Earl Weaver. I went from Yogi to Billy to Earl and was awed by the opportunity to be with these guys. It was the right place at the right time for me.

With the Baltimore Orioles, I experienced the Oriole Way. Cal Ripken Sr. was a coach and a manager during my time there ('86 and '87). His sons, Cal Junior and Billy, were a big part of that. Knowing those guys, playing ball with them, and being around them really showed me a lot about true competitiveness and dedication to baseball.

Cal Junior used to compete in everything in a fun way. He made everything about baseball a game. He and I would pick up balls scattered around the hitting cage after batting practice and race to see who could pick up the most.

I remember taking pre-game infield with him (back when the players took infield), and Cal, who played all those game in a row during a streak that will never be broken, would be at shortstop. If I didn't touch the ground with my glove on a throw from the catcher, Cal would call out, "The runner is safe! No tag. No tag!"

The Oriole Way meant concentrating on the little things, and Junior made it fun. Playing ball with him was a blast. Little did I realize that years later my Angels would be the team playing Cal's Orioles at Camden Yards when he would tie and surpass Lou Gehrig's record for consecutive games played. We were there that September, and I will never forget it. It was great for all of us Angels to have that opportunity.

The night Cal tied Gehrig's record was big. Camera flashes everywhere and forever. The Orioles unveiled that giant banner down that beautiful wall, that big brick warehouse beyond right field: 2131. Move over, Lou. You've got company.

The next day I learned I was in the lineup scheduled to face Oriole ace Mike Mussina. This surprised me. I was a platoon guy. Marcel Lachemann, my manager, only played me against left-handed pitchers, and Mussina was a tough righty. I was excited to see my name in the lineup. Cal was going to break the record, and I heard en route to the ballpark that President Clinton was going to be there, as were Joe DiMaggio and Earl Weaver. Anybody who was anybody would be there. It would be an electrifying evening for everyone in attendance.

We were in a pennant race that year (1995), and it was fun to be in the pennant race; we were trying to win a title for our owner, Gene Autry. But that night the pennant race took second place to playing against Cal. It was a huge night in baseball history, and my teammates were really tight. Thirty minutes before game time, you could hear a pin drop in our locker room. I tried to wake up the troops.

"Hey, fellas," I said, "c'mon, this is just another game. Let's go out and let's attack. We're acting like this is a World Series game. Why is it so quiet in here?"

Looking around the clubhouse, you could tell guys were nervous, very nervous, because soon they'd be taking the field in an historic game with the whole world watching.

Marcel gave me a gift of a lifetime by putting me in that lineup at second base. The baseballs were custom-made for the occasion, laced in orange and stamped with a Cal Ripken Jr. logo and his famous number 8. The balls were counted, numbered, and accounted for. You couldn't just take one. Usually when you sit in the dugout and a ball bounces in, no one bothers to pick it up. In this game, when a ball rolled into the dugout, guys were scrumming for them. Everyone wanted a keepsake.

Even the umpires were specially selected; the ones with seniority got to work the game. Larry Barnett was the dean of American Leagues umps, so he was the home plate umpire. And so it went around the bases.

When my turn came to go up and hit, I wasn't shy. I walked right up to Barnett. "Hey, Larry," I said, "let me have one of those balls in your pocket."

"No, no, no, Hud. You can't have one."

"How am I going to get one?"

"If you're lucky enough to catch a third out, you can have it."

Thanks a lot.

I'm out in the field, there are two outs in the second or third inning, and somebody hits a popup to shallow right field. I'm playing second base, drift back, and wave off (incoming right fielder) Tim Salmon. I'm camped under it.

Salmon calls me off. Outfielders have priority over the infielders, so I have to let him have it. He catches the inning's final out, and as he's running in, I'm running alongside complaining.

"That was my ball! What are you doing? It's unbelievable that you would take that from me!" I added a few more words, spicy ones that need not be repeated.

Salmon has the ball firmly in his glove and says, "Hud, you'll get one."

"Yeah, right."

As the game goes on, I'm really upset about the lost opportunity for my souvenir game ball.

We're trailing, so as soon as we go down to end the top of the fifth, the game is official. Cal's teammates Bobby Bonilla and Rafael Palmeiro push Junior out of the Oriole dugout and insist he take a victory lap. I have never—before or since—seen a player take a mid-game stroll around the field's perimeter to the music of a thunderous, non-stop, packed house, standing ovation.

I was standing at second base in Camden Yards when Bonilla, Palmeiro, and others shove Cal out of the dugout and onto the field. He seems a bit self-conscious and slightly stumbles jogging down the right field line. But once Cal starts down the outfield side of the foul line towards the foul pole, he's reaching out to the fans and giving fives.

I'm still watching from second base as Cal follows the warning track from right field to center. A couple fans fall out of the stands, and he stops to help them back in. This whole time I'm in a dream world. "Wow," I wonder, "is this really happening?"

As Cal reaches the left field corner and turns left toward home, he approaches our dugout. My teammates are standing at the top step applauding, giving love to Cal. I'm out at second base, and I can't do that.

Hey! That's where I want to be! I want to go into the dugout and shake hands with Cal. I want to run in from the field, to get in line. I tell myself, "Self, you don't want to cause a distraction. If you run off the field, people are going to see that. You have to have more respect for the game."

So I stand and watch and miss my opportunity. Cal passes our dugout and is behind home plate with his family. It's too late for Hud.

I'm thinking, "Hud, here you're getting a chance to play in the game, that's great, but you're missing shaking hands. All those guys got pictures, too." I'm kind of bumming.

Once Cal finished his coronation proceeding, I look around. For some reason I'm standing on the pitcher's mound. Right up top, toeing the slab. I've never stood here before.

"Wow," I think, "I'm just going to walk back to my position." I'm in my own little Planet Hud dream world.

How fun that was all that to witness? It was remarkable. Words don't do it justice. I will cherish that moment and retell that story as long as I live.

The field is cleared, and the game resumes in the bottom of the fifth. The Orioles load the bases with two out with Ripken due to hit. Rafael Palmeiro is perched on second as Cal prepares to step in.

Raffy looks at me. "Hud," he says, "isn't it only fitting, in a game like this, Cal comes up with the bases loaded in the fifth inning?"

"Yeah," I said, "it's beautiful."

I retreat to my defensive position at second base and pray.

"God, let me have the ball. Hit it to me."

Shawn Boskie's first pitch to Cal is an inside fastball that jams him. Cal swings and hits a flare over my head toward shallow right-center field.

I take off running. As I'm running, everything suddenly converts to slow motion, like in the movie Chariots of Fire. Or the Bo Derek beach jog in 10.

Break your neck if you have to, but you have to catch that ball.

I keep running. My adrenaline, my speed, takes me to the ball. I catch it on the dead run. I squeeze that third out and can't believe it. I am so excited I shake the ball in my glove. It is like a dream, running after and catching a floating, 10-carat diamond.

The Baltimore fans boo me. The crowd thinks I'm showing up Cal and boo me. I hear them, but they don't understand. I caught my souvenir. I have my baseball.

I run in, having saved a couple runs from scoring, and my teammates are congratulating me.

"Hud, nice catch."

"Way to go, Hud."

I run past them, straight up the steps and into our locker room. I stash the ball in my briefcase. I put it there because I don't want anyone to steal or sabotage my ball or mess with me. Guys do that in baseball, so I hide it somewhere safe. I re-store my briefcase and run back to the dugout.

My teammates razz me big time.

"Hud, what's the deal? You blew us off. We're trying to give you five and everything."

"Here I am right now," I tell them. "Here's a five. I had to take care of my souvenir, man." I am happy as I can be. I got my souvenir right off Cal Ripken's bat the night he broke Lou Gehrig's record.

Throughout my playing career, I collected baseball bats from star players, so my kids would have something when I was done. Cal was always good to other players and always took care of them when asked for an autograph. I asked Cal for an autographed bat a year or so earlier and was pretty blunt about it.

I said, "Hey, Junior! Can I please have one of your autographed bats? I want to put it up on my mantel next to my Pete Rose bat." Pete gave me a bat back in 1988.

Cal is a very smart guy, polite and articulate. He looks at me and says, "Okay, Hud."

But he never gives me a bat. Not then, nor when we returned later in the season to Baltimore. Now, the year he's going to break the record (1995), I see him early in the season and again remind him.

"Hey, Junior, where's the bat you promised me last year?"

"Hud, I forgot. It's coming, it's coming."

So is Santa Claus.

The months roll by, and Pete Rose remains the undisputed king of my mantel.

When we were flying to Baltimore in September for Cal's Lou Gehrig game, I'm sitting next to my good friend Mark Langston. I can't stay quiet for long and prove it.

"Langley," I say, "I've been asking Cal for a bat for a long time. You know what? I think that as classy as that guy is, he's going to sign me a bat this week."

Langston looks at me and says, "Hud, I know you think a lot of yourself. What makes you think Cal Ripken is going to be thinking of you—a little old utility player—on a night when the whole world watches?"

"It's not that I think that much about myself. I know what a class act Cal Ripken is."

The game Ripken ties the record I get no bat. Pete Rose remains alone in my living room.

The game Cal breaks the record we lose. I'm in the clubhouse holding court with 20 media people circled around, dazzling them with my fifth-inning popup story. Up walks a batboy with a bat that he hands to me.

"Here," he says. "This is from the other side."

I take it, look at it, and read what's written in longhand on the barrel: "To Hud, we go a long way back. You going ahead of me in the draft and all. I feel like you feel when you strike out with the bases loaded, visibly shaken. All my best, Cal Ripken."

Junior sent me that bat, right after the game. He saved that bat, so it would be so special; I think he wanted to make sure it would go above the Pete Rose bat, courtesy of a friend who's one of the greatest all-time players ever.

I'm extremely excited Cal and I had that relationship as teammates and, years later, as opponents. That he would take care of me on the biggest night of his professional life like that touched me in a way I'll never forget.

In 21 combined years of playing pro ball—all or parts of 13 in the Big Leagues, and most of 10 in the minors—Cal's record-breaker was the greatest game I ever played in.

If you'll pardon me and excuse my 0–for-4 that night, that game wasn't about anyone but Cal. It celebrated all that was good and right about the game of baseball and the legends who play it best.

Honor the game, and it will honor you. Cal Ripken Jr. is living, walking proof. It was an honor just to be in a game of that magnitude.

❖ All About Hud

Rex Hudler, nicknamed the "Wonder Dog," is a former Major League Baseball utility player. He played all or parts of 13 Big League seasons after being the first round draft pick of the New York Yankees in 1978.

Rex played every position except pitcher for six different Major League teams: the New York Yankees (1984-1985), Baltimore Orioles (1986), Montreal Expos (1988-1990), St. Louis Cardinals (1990-1992), California Angels (1994-1996), and Philadelphia Phillies (1997-1998). He also played for the Yakult Swallows of the Japanese Central League.

After retiring, Hud got into broadcasting. He is a popular color commentator on TV and also for many of the most popular video baseball games. He is president of the non-profit organization Team Up For Down Syndrome, which raises money for public awareness, housing, education, job training, family counseling, and health care for those living with Down Syndrome. Hudler and his wife Jennifer have a son with the affliction.

Rex earned his "Bug-Eater" moniker in St. Louis during a game when he picked an enormous June bug off his hat and was dared to eat it by Cardinal teammate Tom Pagnozzi. The players the dugout got involved and paid Hud $800 to eat the big beetle. He did and pocketed the money.

❖ Hud Quotes

Rex Hudler loves baseball just about as much as anyone and is one of the game's most quotable personalities. Among his gems:

(rhyming) "Cheese on my knees, broke the dish in two. Blew the pitch on by, wouldn't wanna be you!"

"(Manager) Mike (Scioscia) likes to turn (catcher) Bengie (Molina) loose though, so he doesn't get on base and clog the bases."

"You gotta hack, or they'll send you back!"

"That pitch went where he threw it."

(After pitcher Jarrod Washburn had given up 10 runs in four innings) "You gotta give Wash a lot of credit for keeping the bullpen out of it this early."

"All's we need is a walk, a knock, a bloop, and a blast."

"Ummm . . . what are you waiting for, amigo?"

(calling a two-run homer) "Boy, did he drop a huge deuce in the stands!"

(describing a line drive that's really stung) "That's a Screaming Meemie!"

"That bat snapped in two, but it died an Angel hero."

"Be patient, young Jedi!"

"I used to ride the pine for nine."

"These new kids are young, they've got energy. Just give them a PBJ sandwich, and they're good to go!"

"America is the only country in the world where you can go into the grocery store, get whatever you want, put it in the cart, and go home."

❖ Cal Ripken, Junior

Hometown boy makes great. Born and raised north of Baltimore in Aberdeen, the home team drafted Cal with the 48th pick in the 2nd round of the 1978 amateur draft. The team had multiple picks that round and previously had taken Staunton, Virginia high school outfielder Larry Sheets, and San Diego prep pitcher Eddie Hook. Their first choice that year was a Cincinnati high-schooler named Robert Boyce, a third baseman.

Boyce would play four years in the low minors, never rising above Class A ball. He was out of baseball in 1982 at the age of 22.

Also occurring in 1982 in the world of baseball was the explosion of Cal Ripken Junior onto what would eventually become a global stage: 21 seasons including 2,632 consecutive games, 19 consecutive All-Star teams, American League MVP, two-time All-Star MVP, Major League Player of the Year, Lou Gehrig Memorial Award winner, Roberto Clemente Award winner, and lifetime achievement recognition for patiently signing too many thousands of autographs to possibly count.

Ripken honored the game as few have or ever will. He played as hard as he could, as well as he could, at the highest level possible, as long as he could. Since retiring in 2001, his legacy seems to grow by the day.

Cal was ushered into the velvet ropes of the Baseball Hall of Fame in 2007, his first year of eligibility. He earned 98.5 percent of the vote. Fans are left to wonder what the other 1.5 percent was thinking.

Ripken devotes tremendous time and energy in his national youth baseball organization, baseball complex construction business, a very active personal appearance schedule, and teams with brother Bill to champion the Cal Ripken Sr. Foundation in honor of their late father, a legendary Oriole coach and teacher. The brothers invest millions each year helping to build character and teach life lessons to disadvantaged young people in distressed communities.

24

Chris Bosio

Fowl Behavior
in El Paso

We're in El Paso, Texas playing minor league ball, and Terry Bevington is our manager. His brother Zack is the home plate umpire. They have a brotherly love for each other but never got along. Zack was always finding a way to throw Terry out of the game—and Terry usually deserved it.

The San Diego Chicken is in town, the great character mascot developed and perfected by high-energy performer Ted Giannoulas. Ted is doing his typical madcap act throughout the ballgame, and in the fifth inning, Zack throws his brother out of the game for questioning the strike zone.

Terry leaves the field and goes into the clubhouse. Ted is in there. The next inning comes around and the Chicken comes back on the field. He's grown, sprouting from 5'7" to 6'2." His costume is snug. He starts doing the "fat girl or beautiful blond" poster routine, where the fans boo or cheer based on which poster the Chicken holds up. On the ground beside him is a huge water gun.

In El Paso, we have the Diablo Girls dancing on the dugout roof. They are our main gate attraction, along with dollar beer night, dollar Diablo night, and Tony Llama boot night.

After the Chicken finishes his poster routine, the starting pitcher is ready to go. The umpire, Zack, is waiting to resume play, but the Chicken grabs his giant water gun, runs over, and points it right at him.

The Chicken opens fire, starting with the crotch of the umpire's pants and spraying straight up his chest. Then he sprays the ump in his face. Zack is getting really pissed off; none of this is prearranged.

The Chicken is pantomiming his demonstrative belly laugh, and the crowd is loving it. I'm telling you, by the time he finishes, The Chicken has dumped gallons of water on this guy. It was unbelievable. The umpire is totally soaked.

The game resumes, and the next inning rolls around. The opposing pitcher starts complaining because all the baseballs are wet.

The umpire yells out, "My f*$#%! balls are all wet! What do you want me to do?"

The crowd feels offended. One of the fans yells out, "You can't say that here at the stadium."

Bev (Terry, our ejected manager) reappears back out of the clubhouse and walks into our dugout. He comes up to me and asks, "How'd you like the Chicken routine?"

I liked it. "That was awesome," I said.

With a mischievous grin he reveals, "That was me."

Terry was the guy out there unloading on his brother, soaking Zack after getting tossed for arguing balls and strikes. How priceless is that?

Both teams keep griping for the next couple innings because the baseballs are wet, and the fans keep yelling because of all the profanity from the coaches, managers, players, and umpire. Add it all together, and it was a complete cluster.

But because of everything that went on my team had— pardon the pun—a fowl ball.

❖ Ted Giannoulas

A skilled and innovative showman, Ted Giannoulas created his famous San Diego Chicken comedy mascot act while working for a radio station. He volunteered to attend Padres games and quickly became a huge fan favorite. His popularity spread throughout the nation, to the extent that in 1976, Giannoulis was dancing in costume at an Elvis Presley concert and caused Elvis to stop, mid-song, from laughter.

The Chicken grew bigger than the radio station (KGB), and the station fired Giannoulas in May 1979. They tried to block Giannoulas from appearing anywhere in a chicken costume, a lawsuit that ended up going before the California Supreme Court.

The court sided with Giannoulas. He re-hatched himself in an ornate ceremony that unveiled a new costume and signified a new, emancipated beginning as the renamed "Famous Chicken."

Ted Giannoulas has performed at more than 8,500 baseball games and 17,000 public appearances. He signs free autographs for anyone, and everyone who wants one. He has signed an estimated two million, staying as late as 2:20 a.m. at a Texas Rangers game to accommodate his loyal fans.

❖ Chris Bosio

El Paso for Bosio was 1985, his third year in the minors. He would make the Majors the following year and stay with the Brewers through the 1992 season. The spring of 1993 brought a whole lot of chaos to the 30-year-old's life.

Barely a month after his home was robbed by a drifter, close friend Tim Crews drowned in a boating accident, and a woman living below him in Phoenix shot her daughter and killed herself, Chris Bosio's grandfather, to whom Chris was very close, died back home in northern California.

The 1993 season had just gotten underway, and Bosio's first three starts were not validating the four-year, $15 million free agent contract the Mariners dangled to lure him to Seattle.

The fourth start was shaky, too. Bosio walked the first two Red Sox batters to face him. Then he set down 27 in a row, throwing a no-hitter against the Boston Red Sox. It was the second in the history of the Seattle franchise.

25

Ralph Terry

Old Men in the Dugout

When I was 18, I was playing in Binghamton, in the Eastern League, about an hour's ride from Cooperstown. Every year Cooperstown held a benefit game to raise money for the Hall Of Fame, and that year, 1954, the Yankees were playing Cincinnati.

The day of the exhibition, we had an off day in Binghamton, so I drove the hour to Cooperstown to watch the game. The Yankees pitching coach, Jim Turner, got me in the stadium. I was thrilled just to be there.

"Ralphie," he says, "sit on the bench. It's an exhibition game so go sit on the end of the bench with those three old timers." He motions down toward three old guys.

I sit down among them. These guys are pretty old, and I'm a kid, so I'm kind of shy. In the second inning, I turn to the gentleman on my right and introduce myself.

"Hi," I say, sticking out my hand. "Ralph Terry is my name. I'm a pitcher in Binghamton, class A, Eastern League."

"Hi, Ralph," says the old man, taking my hand and shaking it. "Cy Young is my name." He nods toward his two friends and adds, "Shake hands with Zack Wheat and Ty Cobb."

❖ Ralph Terry

Ralph was in the Majors two seasons later, beginning a career that lasted a dozen years and saw him win 107 games. Ralph spent eight years with the Yankees and was 78-59 primarily as a starter. His best season was 1962, going 23-12 with a 3.19 ERA in 298.2 innings of work. He made the AL All-Star team that year but didn't get in the game.

Ralph pitched in five World Series, making nine appearances and six starts while going 2-4. Both of his wins came in 1962 when the Yankees beat the San Francisco Giants. The Bronx Bombers also won the previous season but lost in 1960, 1963, and 1964.

❖ Cy Young

Denton True (Cy) Young pitched from 1890-1911 and won 511 games with a lifetime earned run average of 2.63. A big, strong right-hander, Cy pitched in baseball's dead-ball era and averaged eight innings per each of his 906 appearances. Young posted eleven 20-win seasons plus five more with 30 wins or more. He was voted into 1937's second class for the Baseball Hall of Fame, elected along with Nap Lajoie and Tris Speaker.

❖ Zach Wheat

Zach Wheat was a star leftfielder for the Brooklyn Dodgers for 18 of 19 Major League seasons, batting over .300 14 times with a .317 lifetime average. Wheat played in 2,410 Major League games and scored 1,289 runs while driving in 1,248. He amassed 2,884 hits and was a model of consistency throughout his long career. Eleven times he was in the top 10 in slugging percentage and home runs, and 10 times in the top 10 in hits and total bases. Five years after sitting on that Cooperstown bench next to Ralph Terry, the 1959 Veterans Committee voted Zach Wheat into the Hall of Fame. That summer he was enshrined alongside his friends Cy Young and Ty Cobb.

❖ Ty Cobb

Cobb was the leading vote-getter in the Hall of Fame's initial 1936 five-man induction class, receiving 222 of 226 votes and surpassing (in order) Honus Wagner, Babe Ruth, Christy

Mathewson, and Walter Johnson. Cobb played 22 of his 24 seasons in center field for the Detroit Tigers and amassed 4,189 hits (or 4,191 depending on the source) in only 3,034 games. He scored 2,246 runs and drove in 1,938. Cobb led the American League in 11 offensive categories in 1911 and was voted the league's Most Valuable Player.

Cobb batted .366 for his career and hit .400 two seasons in a row, 1911-12 (.420 and .409). He set 90 Major League records while playing.

Despite the superlative nature of Cobb's unmatched career, he never won a World Series. The Tigers reached it three times but lost all three. He ended up managing for six lackluster seasons and retired from baseball.

Moving back home to Georgia, Ty became a very successful businessman. He later moved to northern California and amassed a great fortune, approximately $90 million in today's present value.

A bittersweet moment in Cobb's life reportedly happened in the late 1940s when Cobb and sportswriter Grantland Rice were returning from watching the Masters golf tournament. The two stopped at a Greenville, South Carolina liquor store and went inside. Cobb recognized the clerk behind the counter as Shoeless Joe Jackson. Jackson had been banned from baseball almost three decades earlier in the wake of the famous 1919 World Series Black Sox betting scandal.

Cobb was sure it was Jackson, but Jackson did not appear to recognize Cobb.

Finally Ty asks, "Don't you know me, Joe?"

Shoeless Joe nodded. "Sure I know you, Ty," he said. "But I wasn't sure you wanted to know me. A lot of them don't."

Ty Cobb's tumultuous life came to a close on July 17, 1961 at Emory University Hospital in Atlanta. He had checked in with a million dollars worth of negotiable bonds and a Luger pistol in a brown paper bag. Cobb's remains are interred at the Rose Hill Cemetery in Royston, a tiny town in Georgia's northeast corner.

26

Mike Scott

Yogi

A couple days before spring training starts, my team, the Houston Astros, is in Kissimmee, Florida getting ready for camp. Pre-spring training routine consists of going to the complex, getting in a light workout, and then heading to the golf course.

Because we are with the Astros, we have access to Lake Nona Golf and Country Club. Lake Nona is one of the two ultra-swank private country clubs featured on the made-for-TV golf exhibition The Tavistock Cup.

On this particular day, I get a group of players together to play some golf, and we drive out to Lake Nona. We get squared away, warm up, and head toward the tee. As we pull our carts up to the first tee box, we see the Astros' coaching staff coming off the course. Yogi Berra, the former Yankee legend who's joined our organization, is among them.

I ask them how they played.

Yogi responds, "I played okay, but I putted (not so good)."

I ask him what was wrong, what happened.

Yogi responds, "They just got done marinatin' the greens."

Maybe it was aerating, maybe it was marinating. Whatever it was, I didn't putt so hot that day either.

❖ More Yogi

Bryant Gumbel, the former host of the Today show, told this particular Yogi story to me at one of our team golf tournaments. As Bryant tells the story, Yogi is a guest on the show (Today).

As his interview with Yogi heads to commercial, Bryant cuts away with, "When we come back, we're going to do a word association with Yogi."

During the commercial timeout, Bryant asks Yogi if he knows what they are going to do. Yogi says he doesn't.

Gumbel explains word association. "I say a word, and you say the first thing that comes to your mind."

Yogi nods and says he understands.

The commercial break ends, the director cues the return to live filming, and Bryant smiles at Yogi and into the camera.

"Alright," he says, "we are back with Yogi Berra. Yogi, we're going to do a little word association."

Yogi nods and says, "Okay."

Bryant says, "Mickey Mantle."

Yogi responds, "What about him?"

❖ Mike Scott

Right-hander Mike Scott threw a no-hitter and struck out 306 men in one season. He went 18-10 with a 2.22 ERA and, despite unproven accusations he was scuffing the baseball, Scott won the 1986 NL Cy Young Award. He won both starts in that year's NLCS, but the Astros lost to the New York Mets in six games. Despite the team defeat, Scott was named series MVP.

Mike's career was not always so successful. He struggled through his first four seasons with the Mets (a combined record of 14-27) and his first two with the Astros (15-17), but everything changed when Roger Craig taught Scott how to throw a split-fingered fastball. That season (1985), Mike won 18 games and signed a rich, new three-year deal. The following year he won the Cy Young. He won 76 games in five seasons, including 20 in 1989.

Late in his career, Scott nearly had a second no-hitter. Ken Oberkfell singled with two out in the ninth to foil the attempt.

After four seasons with the Mets, Scott's final nine were with the Astros. He made three All-Star teams and hit two home runs. He retired in 1991.

❖ Yogi Berra

For a man five-feet-seven to wallop 358 home runs is impressive, regardless when he played. To do it in the post-war era as an everyday catcher is extraordinary. To play 19 seasons, make the All-Star team 15 straight seasons, win three American League MVP awards, and win 10 of 14 World Series means we're talking about only one man: legendary Yankee Hall of Famer Lawrence Peter "Yogi" Berra.

Born in St. Louis in 1925, Yogi signed with the Yankees during World War II. He debuted in the fall of 1946 and quickly produced a body of work unrivaled by any modern day catcher.

Yogi managed the Yankees to a pennant in 1964 at the age of 39. Eight years later, he returned to managing across town and managed the Mets for four years and the 1973 pennant.

Wildly popular throughout his retirement for his innate ability to mangle a phrase and make people laugh, Yogi remains one of the most popular players in the history of the game.

27

Gregg Olson and Brent Mayne

A Very Intentional Walk

❖ Gregg Olson's Perspective

Yes, I was the one who intentionally walked Barry Bonds with the bases loaded to force in a run. No, it was not my idea. Yes, it was the first time it had happened in Major League Baseball in nearly fifty years. No, being a trivia answer is not a career highlight.

I was closing for the Arizona Diamondbacks, and we were on the road in San Francisco. It's raining, we're winning 7-5, there are two out in the bottom of the eighth, and the Giants have a runner on first.

Bonds is announced to pinch-hit for Chris Jones. I enter the game in relief of Amaury Telemaco.

Bonds is patient, and I get behind in the count, three balls and one strike. I decide to snap off a good curveball. If I miss, I walk him and face Brent Mayne.

Drops right in there, strike two. The count is full, and I assume Barry's looking for another breaking ball. I throw him my best fastball down and away, just in case I'm wrong on the breaking ball assumption.

I thought it was a perfect pitch. It's absolute paint, right on the corner.

Ball four, Barry walks. With runners now on first and second, Brent Mayne walks too. Bases loaded.

I strike out Rey Sanchez and escape. The rain falls a little harder.

Dave Dellucci strengthens our friendship by going deep for me in the top of the ninth to boost us to a three-run lead.

In the bottom of the ninth, I walk back out in the rain to face the top of the Giants' order.

Darryl Hamilton strikes out. Good for me, one down and two to go.

Then my mental game starts to erode in concert with my footing. When the mound is wet, my right foot slides a bit on leg lift, and I lose a little concentration on target. Anything that impacts the release point leads to erratic control. The weather qualifies.

I walk Bill Mueller and Jeff Kent, who hits me like it's batting practice, smokes a ground rule double.

Nuts. Runners on second and third, the tying run coming to the plate. I walk the next hitter, Charlie Hayes, to load the bases. This sets up a game-ending double play or a game-ending loss, depending on what happens next.

Stan Javier grounds out to second, so Mueller scores to make it 8-6, but I get my second out. I'm happy to make the trade. Only one more out to go.

Next up is left-handed hitting J.T. Snow. I don't do well against him either and walk him too. I've pitched one official inning and have walked five guys.

The bases are loaded, and, with the game on the line, up saunters Barry Bonds. A single probably ties it, a double probably wins it, and a walk-off and bomb would be, well, I don't even want to think about a bomb.

Short relievers are conditioned for a certain number of pitches. Thirty-five is about the max in a one or two-inning stint. As Bonds digs in, I am already in the mid-40s and have already faced him (last inning) with my best stuff.

Now my velocity is lessening, as is the bite on my breaking ball. Another factor also diminishes a pitcher's stuff: high intensity pitches. I have had the bases loaded three times, and now I am on fumes.

Buck Showalter, my manager, is a very cerebral man and recognizes that I'm done. He steps out of the dugout and holds up four fingers, signaling an intentional walk.

Super. I have to intentionally walk Barry Bonds with the bases loaded. This lets Kent waltz across the plate for free to make it a one-run game. It also advances the tying run to third and the winning run into scoring position.

This is a ballsy move, to say the least. The intentional walk to Bonds is walk number six. I've walked six hitters, and my manager has decided we're better off with the tying run on third.

The next hitter in this destiny escapade is lefty Brent Mayne. I've had mixed success against Mayne throughout our careers; I've gotten him and he's gotten me. Mayne's a good contact hitter and can be a real pain to pitch to.

Sinker, strike one. Curveball, ball one. Changeup, strike two.

Okay, I'm thinking, one good pitch, and I get out of this.

Curveball, ball two.

Still only need one. Changeup, ball three.

Sure, why not? Another full count. Here we go.

He knows what's coming, I know what's coming, and the 12,000 rain-drenched fans know what's coming: sinker, middle of the plate. There is no way I am walking in the tying run.

Foul ball. Foul ball. Foul ball. Foul ball.

And, for good measure, another foul ball.

Five full-count foul balls with the bases loaded. Remember the high intensity pitches I was talking about? Each of these was one.

I wind up, let it fly, and try my best one more time: sinker, middle of the plate.

Mayne rips a liner into right field. I turn and watch my right fielder, Brent Brede, who's right there. Brent lines to Brent, a poetic way to end the game.

Watching, I'm thinking, "Piece of cake."

Wrong. Brede loses it in the lights for a split-second, finds it, and drops to a knee for a dramatic, game-ending catch. I exhale in the rain, half bent over from relief and fatigue. Stick me with a fork, I'm done. D'backs win 8-7.

My teammates and I shake hands and head off the field. Old Candlestick Park has a door down the right field line that opens to a hallway that leads to the 49ers locker room and what used to be the Giants and visitors' clubhouses. The team files through the door. Standing inside the tunnel entrance is

Willie Blair, one of our starting pitchers. Willie is a good ol' boy from Kentucky. He waits, holding two Bud Lights.

He looks at me, hands me one, and says, "Damn, you're fun to watch."

"Thanks," I say. "Give me the beer."

After I ice my body (I would not be available to pitch for three days), I walk into manager Showalter's office.

"Hey, Buck," I say, "next time we walk someone with the bases loaded—and do something that hasn't been done in 47 years—can you at least come out and talk about it?"

"What do you mean?"

"Well, I could have just hit him and saved three pitches."

"I didn't think of that."

"It was a better option. I wouldn't have had to go through the "first guy in 47 years" thing, nobody would have thought I did it on purpose, and Barry would have remembered it the next few times I face him."

"Thanks for the suggestion, Oly. I'll keep it in mind."

Who was he kidding? Buck made the call that won the game. Hats off for the courage it took to make the decision.

It was a dramatic but ugly way to record my sixth save of the year. Check out my line in the box score:

	IP	H	R	ER	BB	SO	HR	ERA
Olson (S, 6)	1 1/3	1	2	2	6	2	0	3.80

Willie's cold beer tasted good that night. If memory serves, I had a second.

* * *

❖ Brent Mayne: Batting after Olson's Bases-Loaded Walk to Barry Bonds

I was catching for the Giants, and we were hosting Arizona. Somehow I ended up hitting behind Barry Bonds. Bonds didn't start that night; he came in to pinch-hit in the bottom of the eighth.

We got some things going and load the bases the next inning, the bottom of the ninth. I'm on deck when Barry walks to the plate. We're down two runs, 8-6, so Barry's got a chance for a walk-off.

Diamondback manager Buck Showalter comes out of the dugout and signals for the intentional walk. They're walking a guy with the bases juiced to force in a run and get to me? Our runner trots across from third, so now it's a one-run game, 8-7.

What am I thinking? I'm thinking it's a bizarre move. But I'm also trying to stay focused. The walk doesn't change my approach. I go to the plate still trying to do the same thing, to get a hit.

It never enters my mind to be upset about it.

I get set in the box, and I'm facing Gregg Olson, who I have faced a lot of times, and we just lock up. I remember fouling off a whole succession of pitches. The battle seems to go on forever. I finally fly out to right field, and it's game over. We lose 8-7.

After the game ended, I was amped up, and my post-game comments were misinterpreted, which created a pretty heavy situation. I wasn't in the greatest of moods, having had a chance to win the game in the ninth but making the final out instead. No pro ever gets used to that. As a hitter, we are only in those situations a handful of times in a career—not every day like a closer.

It wasn't as if I was pissed off at Showalter for disrespecting me. It was just a weird baseball thing that worked, at least for the other guys.

I battled Olson through a long at-bat, pitch after pitch—him trying to do his job, me trying to do mine. In the end, I hit it hard and far. But it just didn't drop.

Truth be told, I'd rather have "sherped" it off the end of the bat for a base hit. Sometimes in baseball it's better to be lucky than good.

* * *

❖ Gregg Olson versus Barry Bonds & Brent Mayne

Olson faced Bonds eight times during his career and walked him four times, twice intentionally. Gregg struck him out once, but Bonds had a single and triple the other three trips.

Brent Mayne hit three singles in 11 lifetime plate appearances against Olson, walking once and striking out once.

❖ Barry Bonds

Baseball's all-time home run leader remains, by far, the most controversial player of his era. His statistics rank among the titans: 762 home runs; 1,996 runs batted in; nearly 3,000 hits (2,935), and 514 stolen bases. What remains hotly debated is how much of that output was steroid-fueled.

Bonds was a 14-time All-Star, 7-time National League Most Valuable Player, 8-time Gold Glover, and 12-time Silver Slugger award winner. His final four MVPs came in succession at the ages of 36-39.

Bonds walked 2,558 times in his career, nearly 1,000 more than Pete Rose and 500 more than Babe Ruth. Bonds walked more than 300 times more often than Rickey Henderson, who ranks second on the all-time list.

Olson's intentional pass was one of Bonds' Major League record 688, but the only one that forced in a run.

❖ Brent Mayne

Brent played for seven teams in his long career, which lasted from 1989-2004. He caught over 1,100 Major League games and is the only catcher in baseball history who won a game as a pitcher. Pressed into an extra-inning of emergency relief with the Rockies, he held the Braves scoreless, the Rockies then scored, and he became the first position player in 32 years to be credited with a victory.

Mayne was a steady left-handed hitter with a .263 lifetime average. An excellent handler of pitchers, in 1991 Brent called and caught Bret Saberhagen's no-hitter for the Royals.

After retiring, Brent parlayed a lot of what he'd learned during his 15 seasons of Major League experience into his first book, called The Art of Catching: The Secrets and Techniques of Baseball's Most Demanding Position. It is an excellent text for coaches, players, aspiring catchers, and fans to better understand the rigors of one of the game's most important defensive positions.

28

Tim Hudson

Ambushing Barry Zito

I started pulling this prank not long after reaching the majors, and it's a beauty.

Whenever a Big League club checks into a hotel during a road trip, everyone's keys are laid out on a table. You walk by, pick up your key, and go up to your room.

Whenever we add someone new to the team, either by a minor league call-up or through a trade, I'd always get off the bus first and get my key. But I also take theirs.

This works with newcomers because they always think, "Well, I'm the new guy, they must have forgotten my key." Then they go back to the front desk and wait to get a new room key. While they're busy doing that, I've already hustled up to their room and entered. I hide in the shower and wait. If I bring an accomplice, I hide in the shower and the other guy hides in the closet, unless we're filming. Then we hide side-by-side.

When our new teammate opens his room with his second key, typically the first thing he does is either hang his coat in the closet or go take a leak.

Can you imagine checking into your hotel room, walking into the bathroom and unzipping your pants to take a leak, and all of a sudden someone jumps out of your shower?

I'm telling you, time and again this maneuver has generated the God-awfulest scream you will ever hear.

We have had some classic victims, really funny ones. The most memorable for me is Barry Zito. Called up just two days before, Zito unlocks his door and walks in after I'm already hidden. He's on his cell phone, talking vintage Zito lingo to one of his buddies back in southern California, describing the Major League life.

"Dude, man," he's saying, "this room's awesome." He's got his head down, pacing the room and talking it up.

I'm sitting in the shower, waiting, eavesdropping, and trying to keep from laughing.

I can hear Barry go to the window, pull the curtains back, and say to his pal, "Dude, you're not going to believe the view I have." Zito is still on the phone when he walks into the bathroom. He unzips his pants and readies to use the commode.

I jump out of the shower. He screams and drops his phone. It lands with a big splash, dead-center in the toilet bowl. This is a perfect hit. Hilarious. The standard by which others shall be measured.

Over the past couple seasons, David Ross and I have teamed up, and now we take a video camera. I have video-taped eight or ten of these ambushes. David hides beside me in the shower.

I often wear a mask. Remember the movie Scream? I have the Scream mask. I also use a mask of a very old man. We have some really exciting footage scaring guys. I just wish we had Zito.

❖ Tim Hudson

Oakland's sixth-round draft choice out of Auburn in 1997, Hudson was starting in the Major Leagues two years later and has been winning ever since. The talented right-hander won 11 or more games in 12 of his first 13 seasons and has compiled an outstanding record of 181-97. Hudson was 20-6 in 32 starts in 2000 and is a three-time All Star.

Originally from Columbus, Georgia, Tim was traded from Oakland to Atlanta for three players in the winter of 2004. He has made it to the postseason five times but has yet to advance out of the Divisional playoffs.

❖ Barry Zito

Oakland's first round pick in the 1999 draft, Zito made it to the Majors and got scared in the bathroom the very next year. The big lefty joined right-hander Hudson in the A's starting rotation, and the pair was the heart of Oakland's staff from 2000-04. Both were dominating aces and teamed to produce a masterful 153-77 won/loss record.

Zito won 133 games his first 10 Major League seasons and is 4-3 in seven lifetime postseason starts. A three-time All Star, Barry earned the American League Cy Young Award in 2002 after going 23-5 with a 2.75 ERA and leading the league in victories.

After seven seasons with Oakland, Barry signed as a free agent with the San Francisco Giants, switching leagues and moving across the bay. He is still searching for similar success.

29

Gregg Olson

Hi, Sparky!

Team fights are never good. Baseball players are not like hockey players. We like teeth and don't like blood. Grown men wrestling in spikes do not create poetic ballet.

During my career, I ran out of the bullpen for a dozen or so fights. In most, no punches were thrown. When you're out in the bullpen, running in is a sense of duty. Dugout guys get there first, so by the time bullpenners reach the mound, it's usually cleanup duty.

But when something happened and I did have to run in to bond with the boys, I always laughed at who I was paired with.

In a fight against Oakland, I got Mark McGwire. Against Toronto, I get circled by Duane Ward and Tom Henke. Both of those guys are 6'5" or so with muscles that weigh around 230.

Nothing happened either time, but these are not the match-ups you look forward to after running 100 yards to hug in the fray.

I did have one matchup that I really thought would have been advantage me. I was with the Orioles, we were home against Detroit at Camden Yards, and one inning earlier a batter on my team got hit.

Detroit comes to the plate, and Mike Mussina hits Tony Phillips on the back foot with a breaking ball. Phillips charges the mound, and a fight begins.

I pace myself on the jog in from the outfield bullpen, and by the time I arrive, the scrum is ending. There's not much to do except stand behind the mound and look for someone to pull off the pile. I also keep glancing around to make sure I

117

don't get cheap-shotted from behind. Prevention, of course, is a veteran's best alternative.

Somebody grabs me by the shirtsleeve. I spin around like Jackie Chan, ready to strike, and see a familiar face. It's Detroit manager Sparky Anderson. I say hello.

"Hey, Sparky."

"Oles, what the f*$#%! are we doing out here?"

His question is relevant to both of us. Neither of us has a clue why Phillips would charge the mound after being hit on the foot with a breaking ball.

"I have no idea, Sparky."

"Well," he says, "I have you."

I'm good with that. If something happens, he and I have just agreed to lock up if a fight resumes.

"Alright," I say, "me and you." I grab his jersey sleeve and give it a tug.

The fight does not resume, so the field is soon cleared. Sparky goes back to his dugout, and I make the long march back behind the centerfield wall to our bullpen.

As far as fights go, this is a good one. It was nice to dance and chat for 10 minutes with a Hall of Fame manager.

❖ Gregg Olson

Gregg saved 160 games his first five full Major League seasons and gave up just 10 home runs against 1,463 batters. Early in 1992, barely three years into his career, Olson became the youngest pitcher (25) to record 100 saves. Arm troubles plagued him beginning at the tail end of the 1993 season and haunted him for the remaining eight years of his career.

❖ George "Sparky" Anderson

The pride of Bridgewater, South Dakota, Sparky Anderson managed three World Series champions, back to back in 1975-76 with the National League's Cincinnati Reds and again in 1984 with the American League Detroit Tigers.

Sparky had very limited skills as a player and made it to the Majors for just one season, 1959, with the Philadelphia Phillies. In 152 games, he hit just .218 with nine doubles, three triples, and zero home runs. He stole six bases and was caught nine times.

Sparky stood 5'7" and weighed 170 pounds, so for Olson he was a great guy to partner with while others threw each other around.

While his playing career was brief, Sparky Anderson soared as a Major League manager. He won five pennants and three world titles in 26 seasons, his first pennant in his first season at age 36. He went on to win nearly 55 percent of 4,030 games before retiring at the age of 61.

Twenty times Sparky's teams finished above .500, and twice he was named American League Manager of the Year. The Veterans Committee voted George "Sparky" Anderson into the Baseball Hall of Fame in 2000. He was enshrined in Cooperstown that summer along with Carlton Fisk and Tony Perez, as well as 1880's infielder Bid McPhee and longtime Negro League outfield star Turkey Stearnes.

Sparky passed away at the age of 76 in Thousand Oaks, California.

30

Mark Lemke

Bedrock & Harry Caray

In 1993 Steve Bedrosian made our Atlanta Braves ballclub and he was fired up. Bedrock had been out of baseball for a year or so and came into camp in really great shape. From the moment he arrived, he was ready to go.

We open the regular season with a series in Chicago against the Cubs, and Bedrock gets called in to relieve in one of our first games. During his warm-up pitches, Bedrock is pumping away, his adrenaline is flowing, and he's throwing 100 miles per hour.

But his final warm-up pitch gets away, Bedrock firing it way high. The ball sails over the backstop, hitting and ricocheting off the very top of the net behind home plate and up near the press box in Wrigley Field.

Bedrock storms around the mound like he always did, the look of a lion in his eyes. After the catcher throws the ball down to second base, I end up with the baseball after our infield throw-around and decide to walk the ball to the mound to hand it to him.

"Hey, Rock," I say, "way to go. What happened on that last pitch?"

"I went up and in on Harry Caray!"

As it turns out, that wild pitch of Bedrock's wasn't so wild after all. Bedrock was pretending to brush back legendary Cubs sportscaster Harry Caray, who was up in the press box, pretty darn close to where Bedrock's last pitch ricocheted.

A bit high, maybe. But Bedrock got Harry's attention.

❖ Steve Bedrosian

After winning the NL Cy Young Award in 1987 as a closer for the Phillies, Bedrock was out of baseball in 1992 before returning in '93. He had an excellent season as a set-up man, going 5-2 with a career best 1.63 ERA in 49 appearances. He gave up only 34 hits in 49 2/3 innings of work.

❖ Harry Caray

Harry Carabina was a very popular Hall of Fame baseball broadcaster whose Chicago presence was magnified into a national one by cable television superstation WGN, which carried the Cubs. Earlier in his career Harry called games for the St. Louis Cardinals, Oakland A's, and the Chicago White Sox before moving to the Cubs after the 1981 season. His career began with the Cardinals in 1945, in concert with the end of World War II.

Born to a poor immigrant family in an impoverished area of St. Louis, both of Harry's parents died before he was 10. Despite a difficult childhood, he ended up becoming a folk hero to American baseball fans from coast to coast. Because of his immense popularity in Chicago and high profile downtown after games, Harry was fondly called "The Mayor of Rush Street."

Harry Caray loved baseball from an early age and played semipro ball before opting into the radio business at age 19. Once in it, he stayed in the business for more than 50 years.

Up until the very end of his career, Harry implored Cub fans to sing loud and loyally during the seventh inning stretch to his signature, off-key rendition of "Take Me Out to the Ballgame."

Harry Caray died in 1998 and is interred at All Saints Cemetery in Des Plaines, Illinois. A large statue of Harry, urging Cub fans to sing, stands on the concourse outside his beloved Wrigley Field.

31

George Brett and Jamie Quirk

July 24, 1983: the Pine Tar Incident

❖ George Brett's Version:

As famous as the game became, I don't remember much about what happened in the first eight innings, but I do remember U. L. Washington coming up late in the game: the top of ninth with two out, and Goose (Gossage) is pitching.

U. L. singles to left, and I'm up. I've had some success versus Goose in the past but not a lot. I hit a home run off him in 1980 to win the playoffs. Prior to that, I hadn't done that much against him, but I had that success in the memory bank.

Shane Rawley had started the game for the Yankees, and I had gotten a hit or two off of Shane. Gossage threw harder than Rawley, and I hit the first pitch I saw home run distance but foul.

When Goose pitches against right-handers, he throws some sliders. But I'm a lefty. Mostly Goose is just, "Hey, I'm going to throw it as hard as I can. If you hit it, congratulations—I hope you hit it at somebody. If you don't, good job."

More bluntly he'd say, "I'm going to throw it as hard as I can, and if you can't hit it, sit the f*$#%! down." That was Goose's thing. He was a power guy, not a finesse guy.

I foul a pitch way down the first base line, and he throws a heater up and in. For some reason, I don't know why, I swing at it. It was a tough pitch to hit. I tomahawk the hell out of it and hit a home run into the right field seats.

I'm running the bases and oblivious to what's going on at home plate. Billy Martin has already grabbed the bat from the batboy. The batboy ran out to get it, and Billy came running out to intercept him. I've watched video of it: I'm crossing home plate, Billy is out there talking to the umpire, and the umpire is holding my bat. The batboy is waiting nearby.

I'm thinking, "What the hell is going on here?"

I go back inside the dugout, stand for a while, and then sit down because Billy and the ump are talking for a good 10 minutes. I'm sitting next to Frank White and Vida Blue and Frank says, "They might call you out for using too much pine tar on your bat."

Billy Martin is walking back to home plate with the umpiring crew. Home plate umpire Tim McClelland is holding my bat. Nick Bremigan, Joe Brinkman, and Drew Coble join Martin and McClelland, and McClelland lays the bat across the plate.

I'm mystified. What is that about?

Someone in the dugout near me, I think it's Frank, says, "They are probably measuring the pine tar."

The rule was that you could only have pine tar up to 18 inches from the handle toward the label. Since the plate is 17 inches across, the umpires wanted to see how much I had.

I had used that bat for a long time without breaking it. The Yankees had visited us in Kansas City two weeks prior, and I was using it then. Good wood is always judged by grain; the thicker the grain, the better the bat. That bat had eight pieces of grain, that's it. It was the best bat I had ever seen.

I used that bat but didn't do anything special in that three-game series in Kansas City. Nothing I did determined the outcome of any of those games, so they (the Yankees) didn't say anything about my bat.

Now, two weeks later, we're playing in Yankee Stadium, and I do exactly that: I hit a home run at a crucial time.

Graig Nettles is the guy who told Billy Martin I was using an illegal bat. The Yankees didn't do anything when I got a hit in the first inning or another one in the fifth inning. They were waiting for something big, and, sure enough, I gave it to them.

When McClelland laid the bat down across the plate, Frank (White) said, "I think they're going to call you out."

I said, "If they call me out, I'm going to run out and kill one of those son-of-a-bitches."

I swear, the split-second I said the word bitches, Tim McClelland picks up the bat, says something to the other umpires, and looks over to our dugout. He's looking for me. McClelland has my bat in his hand, he points to me—almost like he's saying, "Oh, there you are"— and signals and says, "You're out!"

That's when I catapulted out of the dugout. To this day, it's kind of funny because Tim (McClelland) and I are good friends, and I get along well with all the umpires. Obviously, that day I didn't. I come running out and get right in his face, pointing my finger at McClelland. Base umpire Joe Brinkman comes up from behind, grabs me around the neck, and starts pulling me back. I don't know who's got me, and I struggle to get away.

That's what makes watching it look so bad. The more I struggle to escape Brinkman, the more Brinkman pulls back. Several people rush to get between me and Tim McClelland. Dick Howser (my manager) is out there, John Wathan is out there, and Joe Simpson grabs me as soon as Joe Brinkman lets go. Simpson pushes me back, farther away like a good teammate would do.

A funny thing that happened next. Gaylord Perry was on our team that year, and Gaylord's known as a pretty good memorabilia collector. Gaylord decides he's going to steal the bat. He walks out and takes the bat from Tim McClelland. Just takes it, like it's his, and he wants it back.

Gaylord runs off with it, and someone starts after him. Gaylord tosses the bat to Steve Renko. Renko now has the bat and doesn't know what to do with it, so he gives it to someone else, who takes off running up to our locker room.

Suddenly everyone wants the bat. You have all the New York police that are on the field, the security guys, the umpires, Gaylord Perry . . . everyone wants it. Orders go out over walkie-talkies: "Lock the clubhouse! Someone has the bat, and he's running up the tunnel! Do not—I repeat, do not—let him in the clubhouse!"

The all-points bulletin worked. After all that trouble, the umpires finally retrieve the bat.

Our manager, Dick Howser, doesn't care. He is still screaming mad, and I am hyperventilating from all the yelling. I remember leaving the field, to get my glove and hat, and I see (umpire Nick) Bremigan standing there. He's talking to somebody, and I just start mother-f-bombing him: "You gutless motherf*$#%! . . ."

Howser butts in. Joe Simpson grabs me again and tells me that I've done enough. I got kicked out of the game, but I never got suspended, never got fined.

The bat is sent to American League President Lee MacPhail's office on Park Avenue in Manhattan. After two or three days, Lee rules that the bat had nothing to do with me hitting a home run. He said the rule was old, written back in the old days because teams didn't have a lot of bats or baseballs. When a player would get a crack in his bat, he often put finishing tacks in the bat and nailed the wood back together. Then he covered it with pine tar to keep the repair together. Players used bats for so long that pine tar would creep up, and every time a ball was hit on the barrel, the tar smudged the baseball. They'd have to throw the ball out, and baseballs were scarce. That's why they came up with the 18-inch rule.

Two months later, we have to go to Baltimore to play the Orioles but have an off day on the trip and so do the Yankees. Since Lee MacPhail ruled in our favor, we had to return to New York, resume after my at-bat, and finish the ninth inning. They are home, finishing is easy. For us it's more complicated. We have to deviate to a stop in New York, get all the equipment off the plane, go to Yankee Stadium, dress and warm up, play four outs, take a shower and change, drive back to LaGuardia, and then fly down to Baltimore.

Since I was kicked out the first time for arguing, I'm not even allowed to go to the stadium.

The game restarts, two outs in the top of the ninth, I don't remember who's pitching now for the Yankees. I think they had Mattingly playing second.

When the game resumes, Hal McRae bats after me, so he is up next. Hal makes our last out.

The Yankees come to bat in the bottom of the ninth, and (our closer Dan) Quisenberry comes in. Two groundballs and a popup, and that's it. Game over, we win again.

While my teammates are doing all this, I am sitting inside a little Italian restaurant near LaGuardia with Larry Ameche, our TWA sales rep. We always flew TWA charters, and Larry is actor Don Ameche's son. With hours to fill thanks to the trip's logistics, we ended up getting shit-faced at the bar.

He and I are watching the game on television. Larry knew how long it would take the ballclub to get from the stadium to the airport, so we timed it to return to the plane just before the team did. We were a bit early. By the time the team arrived, Larry was asleep, out cold.

I sold the bat once but ended up buying it back. It seemed everybody wanted it. All these people were calling, all of these collectors. Back in the mid-eighties was when interest exploded in collecting and selling autographs. Part of it was because there wasn't a lot of memorabilia available. I sold it to Barry Halper, the most famous collector of all. Halper was a minority owner of the New York Yankees, and his was the biggest and best collection of anyone except for the Hall of Fame in Cooperstown.

John Wathan and I were invited to visit Barry's house in New Jersey when we were in town playing the Yankees. We went, and it was amazing.

Halper had a pushbutton dry cleaning rack, the kind they use when you go to the cleaners to pick up your stuff. He opened a picture, moved it off the wall and behind it, he had a book with every uniform in his collection.

He'd say, "What uniform do you want to see?"

Wathan or I could name just about anybody, and he'd look it up, press the button, and the uniforms would rotate around the track until the one wanted arrived, and he'd stop it. There it is. You name it, Halper had it. The racks went all throughout his house, but the only place it was displayed was in his memorabilia room. It was the damnedest collection I had ever seen.

So I sold the bat to Halper for twenty-five grand, just to get rid of it. The pine tar game wasn't the last time I used it; I used it again after I got it back and probably would have kept using it if Gaylord Perry hadn't told me that if I broke it, it's no longer valuable.

So I quit using it and sold it. One month later, I bought it back from Halper for the same amount, twenty-five grand, because I didn't feel good about selling it. In exchange, I sent him another game-used bat. I ended up giving the pine tar bat to Cooperstown. The bat is on display there.

One week after the original chaos, we are playing in Detroit, and Tim McClelland is umpiring home plate. I had just gotten my bat back from Lee MacPhail's office in New York. They shipped it to me Emery Express, and I walk up to the plate with it in the first inning.

I used a 34-inch bat and rubbed it down sixteen inches with rubbing alcohol. I drew a little red line on it and rubbed it down, so my bat was pure pine tar for 18 inches, and the next 16 inches was beautiful wood. I cleaned it, removing all the excess pine tar. All that work, and then Gaylord tells me I can't use that bat.

I go up to home plate, and McClelland asks, "Hey, George, you want me to check for pine tar?"

I said, "Timmy, let's just let this thing ride a little bit."

I've done a lot of banquets with Tim McClelland; I just happen to be in town, and he's there. A lot of times people get the two of us together to talk about that game.

Timmy has said, "George acts really tough on the field. I wanted to see what he was going to do if Joe Brinkman didn't grab him. I'm 6-feet-6, I have shin guards on, and I have a chest protector. I have a bat in one hand and a mask in the other. George, what were you going to do to me?"

Tim's still umpiring. You look back on his career, he had Sammy Sosa when the cork flew out of Sammy's bat; he was the home plate umpire for that. He had another illegal bat too, maybe Albert Belle. Sammy's excuse was a beauty: he used the corked bat during batting practice to impress the fans at Wrigley Field.

Like you need a corked bat to impress the fans of Wrigley Field? The gates aren't open for batting practice, and the fans aren't even in the ballpark when the home team is hitting.

It doesn't make sense to me either.

❖ Teammate Jamie Quirk's Version:

We're noticing something weird. Nettles is playing third for the Yankees and talking to the nearby umpire. The umpire Nettles talks to goes to home plate to talk to home plate umpire Tim McClelland. None of us think they are going to check the pine tar.

The next thing we know, Yankee manager Billy Martin is coming of the dugout to talk to the umpires. That was when we knew something was up.

One of the guys says, "Wait a minute, they're gonna check his bat."

The drama kept building and building. And what made it really great was that back then there was no fence in front of the dugout (like they all have now). Back then you could just fly out of the dugout, like George did.

We're all just sitting there in the dugout watching all this unfold, and the next thing we know, George launches off the bench and goes flying out there. He probably told you, he has an absolute hate for the Yankees. We'd been in the playoffs with them multiple times, had some fights with them. Any time he did something against the Yankees, he doubled his pleasure because he just loved beating the Yankees.

When George saw Billy Martin come out and check the bat, he just flipped out. We've all seen the video. He's just sitting there, fuming because they're even thinking about checking the bat. Then McClelland raises his hand to call him out, and George comes flying out.

Great player, great play, great theater, great memory. For all that, we can thank George.

❖ More About the Famous Game:

The Royals were trailing 4–3 with two outs in the top of the ninth and U. L. Washington on first base. George Brett homers off fellow future Hall of Famer and Yankee reliever Goose Gossage for a two-run home run to give Kansas City a 5–4 lead.

As Brett crossed the plate, New York manager Billy Martin asks home plate umpire Tim McClelland to check Brett's bat. Martin and other Yankees had noticed its excessive amount of pine tar but chose not to say anything until the home run. Yankees third baseman Graig Nettles recalled a similar incident eight years earlier involving teammate Thurman Munson.

With Brett watching from the dugout, McClelland and the rest of the umpiring crew inspect the bat and determine the pine tar exceeds what's permitted under Rule 1.10(b), which reads "a bat may not be covered by such a substance more than 18 inches from the tip of the handle."

McClelland searches for Brett in the visitors' dugout, points at him, and signals that he is out, his home run doesn't count, and the game over. The Yankees win 4-3.

Brett storms out of the dugout and has to be physically restrained from the umpire. As one writer later noted, "Brett has become the first player in history to hit a game-losing home run."

The Royals protested the game, and their protest was heard by American League President Lee MacPhail. MacPhail overruled McClelland's decision and restored Brett's home run, saying pine tar on bats did not create an unfair advantage. Since Brett had not violated the spirit of the rules nor deliberately "altered [the bat] to improve the distance factor," the bat should have been simply removed from the game and play resumed.

MacPhail ordered the game to be finished, starting with two out in the top of the ninth inning, and the Royals leading 5–4. Brett was ejected for his outburst. Royals' manager Dick Howser was also ejected, and Gaylord Perry was ejected for conspiring to hide the bat in the clubhouse.

The Yankees counter-appealed to no avail. On August 18 (a scheduled off day for both teams), the game was resumed with 1,200 fans in attendance. Yankee manager Billy Martin symbolically protested by putting Ron Guidry (a starting pitcher) in center field and veteran lefty first baseman Don Mattingly at second base. He played the game under protest.

Yankees reliever George Frazier struck Hal McRae out to end the top of the ninth, twenty-five days after the game had begun. Relief ace Dan Quisenberry retired New York in order in the bottom of the ninth to close the Royals' 5–4 win.

The pine tar bat has been on display at the Baseball Hall of Fame in Cooperstown since 1987. The home run ball Brett hit was caught and sold by journalist Ephraim Schwartz to collector Barry Halper for $500 plus 12 Yankees tickets. Gossage later signed the pine tar ball, "Barry, I threw the fucking thing."

Schwartz also gave Halper his ticket stub, and Halper also acquired the can of Oriole Pine Tar from which Brett coated his bat.

The game's winning pitcher was reliever Mike Armstrong, who went 10–7 in 58 appearances. In a 2006 interview, Armstrong said an angry Yankees fan stood on an overpass after the game and threw a brick that cracked the team bus windshield as the Royals left for LaGuardia Airport.

❖ George Brett

George Brett was born to hit a baseball. By the time he retired, George owned the Major League record for hits by a third baseman (3,154). He got all of them with the Royals, the only team he ever played for.

During the 1980 season, George batted .390 and was hitting .407 as late as August 25.

A 1999 inductee into the Baseball Hall of Fame at Cooperstown, Brett is one of only four Major League stars to amass 3,000 or more hits and 300 home runs, and maintain a lifetime batting average of .300 or more.

For that achievement, he remains in very select company. The other three are Willie Mays, Stan Musial, and Hank Aaron.

Today George has significant ownership stakes in several minor league baseball franchises as well as the Spokane Chiefs of the Western Hockey League.

❖ Jamie Quirk

An all-state quarterback at St. Paul High School in Whittier, California, Quirk was offered a football scholarship at Notre Dame but turned it down to sign with the Royals when chosen 18th in the first round of the 1972 draft. Taken four spots in front of him was lefty Scott McGregor, a prep pitcher from nearby El Segundo High School, who would go on to an All-Star career that saw him win 138 games for the Baltimore Orioles. Four spots behind Quirk went Chet Lemon, another L.A. area prepster taken 22nd by the Oakland Athletics. Lemon was a three-time All-Star who played 16 seasons for the Chicago White Sox and Detroit Tigers.

Quirk played longer than any of them, wearing 10 uniform numbers while playing for eight teams over 18 seasons. He would spend three tours of duty and 11 seasons in Kansas City.

A solid catcher and left-handed pinch-hitter, in late-September the year after the famous Pine Tar game, Quirk hit a game-winning home run in his only plate appearance for the Cleveland Indians, beating Minnesota. The Twins loss gave his former team, the Royals, a two-game divisional lead with three games to play. The Royals would clinch the division the following day but were swept in three straight games by Sparky Anderson's powerful Detroit Tigers.

The next year, 1985, Quirk would return to Kansas City. The Royals beat the St. Louis Cardinals in seven games that fall to win the World Series, but Quirk did not see action.

He retired as a player in 1992 and went on to become a Major League coach.

Quirk and Brett remain very close friends.

32

Chris Bosio

A Steak at Stake: Ken Griffey Jr. vs. Lou Piniella

I was at spring training with the Seattle Mariners at the Peoria Sports Complex in Arizona in, I think, 1995. Rafael Soriano was a young pitcher, just coming up, a hard-throwing kid whose fastball ranged from 93 to 97 miles per hour.

On our first day of live batting practice, Jay Buhner, Ken Griffey Jr., and Edgar Martinez rotate through the cage to face him. Buhner steps in first. Jay is a good fastball hitter. He hits a couple of line drives but barely fouls several that bounce off the top of the cage.

This kid on the mound is impressive; he starts to get people's attention.

Edgar Martinez, one of baseball's best right-handed batters and best-ever designated hitters, is known for tracking pitches early in spring training. He replaces Buhner in the cage. Edgar stands at the plate tracking seven or eight fastballs. He doesn't swing, just watches, and studies the velocity and ball flight of each pitch to help sharpen his timing.

Soriano is throwing 94-95 miles per hour, the mitt is popping, and more teammates walk over to watch. The gathering crowd and sounds quickly draw manager Lou Piniella's attention.

Ken Griffey Jr. replaces Edgar in the cage, and Junior's trying to dial it up. Griffey goes into that Junior waggle, swings at the first pitch, and fouls the ball inside the cage. He swings again: another foul dribbler in the cage. His swing is

133

late; a left-handed hitter, Griffey's fouling balls toward the third base side.

Soriano rifles in a third heater, which Griffey again fouls off. None have advanced out of the cage.

Piniella yells out, "Junior, I'll bet you a steak dinner that you can't get a ball out of the cage."

Junior replies, "You're on, Skip."

Soriano throws three more pitches, and Junior swings through two of them, missing both cleanly. He fouls back the other.

The Griffey-Piniella wager comes down to one final pitch. Junior fouls that one off in the cage, too.

"You owe me a steak dinner," Piniella calls out.

"You got it, Skip."

The next morning I arrive at the park and walk inside the clubhouse. It's early, but a powerful stench permeates the air. Clubhouse guys are scurrying all over, and more media guys are around than usual. I go to my locker and ask one of the fellows, "What's going on around here? Something's up. What's up?"

He points down the hall, toward Lou's office. I start heading that way but stop. Guys are whispering to get ready, that Lou is coming in.

Junior (Griffey) is waiting, as are the rest of us, when Piniella walks in. Lou looks around the room. We all look back. None of us should be eyeballing the manager, because none of us are having a very good spring,

Lou barks, "What are you guys looking at? Let's go! Let's win a ballgame today."

Everybody gathers in the hallway near Lou's office. I move closer too, and when I do, I notice the flies—a whole lot of flies. Too many. Flies are everywhere. There are so many flies, the air is thick with them. It's unbelievable.

At this point, I still don't know what's going on, but one of the guys tells me to move closer, to stand by Lou's office. I do, just as Lou walks down the hall and pauses by his office door. Thirty guys rush to get behind him, filling the hallway, crowding and shoving toward Lou's office.

Lou opens his door. Junior is waiting inside, flanked by camera guys and beat writers. Also waiting to say hello is a 1,500-pound steer with crap caked all over its body. Cow pies all over Lou's carpet. Flies are everywhere, several of them buzzing the poop stuck to the steer's ass.

Lou is nearly speechless. All he can manage is, "Holy shit."

Beaming broadly, Griffey pats the steer on the rump and says, "Here's your steak dinner, Skip."

The clubbies try to *moove* the steer out of Lou's office, which proves to be quite an ordeal. The steer is in no particular hurry to leave the air-conditioned comfort of Lou's office, and it takes a whole of lot of bovine engineering to get the big fellow to move.

The steer does not go peacefully, dropping more manure bombs as it plods down the hallway. The scene it leaves behind is ghastly. Manure is everywhere—even stuck to the wall—and there are too many flies to count, celebrating manure wherever they find it, which is pretty much anywhere they look.

That's the story of the steak dinner payout in the batting cage bet between Lou Piniella and Ken Griffey Jr.

Piniella won—sort of—but Griffey got the last laugh.

❖ Chris Bosio

Chris Bosio pitched 11 seasons in the Majors, the first seven for the Milwaukee Brewers, the final four for the Seattle Mariners. A second round pick in the January 1982 secondary amateur draft, Bosio signed out of high school and steadily progressed through the minors. He reached the Majors in August 1986, at the age of 23.

A big, powerful, right-handed starter, Chris won 94 games in his career and five times he won 10 or more in a season.

Over the two-year span of 1990-91 with the Brewers, Chris was 30-16 and won nearly half of his 65 starts. Bosio was a reliable and durable starter; he averaged seven innings per start who kept the ball in the park. He surrendered just 162 homers in 1,710 innings of work.

As a footnote to Bosio's career, on June 6, 1993 he and Baltimore's Mike Mussina got tangled up in a beanball war that caused a real on-field brawl between the Mariners and Orioles. Injured during the fight was Oriole legend Cal Ripken Junior, then two years shy of Lou Gehrig's consecutive game streak. Ripken wrenched his knee and was left with severe pain and swelling.

When he broke the record two years later, Ripken said, "It was the closest I've come to not playing."

❖ Ken Griffey Junior

A living legend, Ken Griffey Jr. spent the first 11 of his 22 Major League seasons with the Seattle Mariners. His accumulated offensive statistics include 630 home runs and 5,271 total bases. A lifetime .284 hitter, Griffey amassed 2,781 hits and drove in 1,836 runs. His career slugging percentage is .538.

Ken Griffey Jr. will always be remembered by those who played with and against him—or watched him—as a five-tool star of consummate skill who kept the integrity of the game above personal self-interest.

Competing throughout the tumult and cheating dishonesty of baseball's steroid era, Griffey refused to partake. His numbers were earned fair and square—some say the hard way—during a time when many other baseball sluggers willingly chose to inflate themselves and their statistics with performance enhancing drugs.

Thirteen times an All-Star and MVP of the 1992 game, Ken was awarded 10 Gold Gloves for defensive excellence. He was the American League's Most Valuable Player in 1997 and slugged 56 home runs in back-to-back years (1998-99).

Ken Griffey Jr. played in the postseason three times. He never made it to the World Series.

❖ Lou Piniella

An outstanding pro hitter for 18-year seasons, Lou played the outfield and was a career .291 hitter who reliably made contact. Lou played entirely in the American League and was consistently productive throughout his 11 seasons with the New York Yankees. In nearly 6,400 plate appearances, Lou had more than three times as many hits (1,701) as strikeouts (541). He was also a clutch performer in the postseason, with a .305 career postseason average in 10 series. Lou delivered 13 hits for the Yankees in their back-to-back World Series wins of 1977-78.

Long considered one of baseball's most volatile and excitable personalities, Lou's long playing career transitioned into an even longer career as a Major League manager. In 1990, Piniella managed the Cincinnati Reds to the World Series championship. He skippered five ball clubs for 23 seasons and retired in 2010. He is now more cautious when betting steak dinners.

33

Jack Howell

Happy Birthday, Jimmie Reese

When I broke into the Majors with the California Angels, Wally Joyner and I were the big rookies. Wally was going to be the new first baseman, and I was due to take over at third. All Wally had to do was replace one of the greatest hitters of all time, future Hall of Famer Rod Carew. I had to replace another solid pro, Doug DeCinces.

Jimmie Reese, a living legend in baseball circles to so many players, was one of our coaches. Jimmie had been Babe Ruth's old roommate back in the early 1930s with the Yankees. Jimmie would be in professional baseball a remarkably long time—nearly 80 years—and was an extremely popular fellow. Everyone knew him and loved him.

Whenever we had batting practice, Jimmie would walk out the outfield with his fungo bat and hit fungos to us. He was really old even then, back when Wally and I arrived on the scene, but he was still a true fungo master, an artist with the thin stick. He could hit the ball with amazing control, pretty much exactly as he wanted.

Jimmie lived into his nineties, but back when Wally and I were breaking in, he was just turning eighty-five and with us at practice on his eighty-fifth birthday. Being the team's young rookie leaders, Wally and I decided we needed to do something special for Jimmie's birthday—maybe a dancer or a stripper.

With Wally being a Mormon and me being the ballclub's chapel leader, we called a singing telegram company to send someone to the locker room and do something special. I remember telling the girl who called us back that we needed to keep it clean. We told her Jimmie was an old guy, and we needed to be careful with whatever we did.

After batting practice, Wally and I gathered everyone together in the locker room. We place a chair in front and had Jimmie take a seat; the rest of us were going to sing "Happy Birthday."

All of a sudden there's a loud bang on the clubhouse door. One of the guys goes and opens it and in walks a girl in a police uniform carrying a music box. The girl marches up, turns on the boom box, plays her music, and starts gyrating.

Then she stops just long enough to handcuff Jimmie to the chair.

Wally and I are terrified. Seeing Jimmie handcuffed to that chair, we worry he'll have a heart attack. Here's Wally Joyner, the young Mormon kid, and me, the chapel leader, bringing in a dancer that possibly gives 85-year-old Jimmie Reese a heart attack instead of a birthday cake.

Thankfully the girl keeps it clean, and nothing bad happens. It was nice to see Jimmie's eyes grow as wide as they could. Wally and I never had the guts to ask, but I think he enjoyed it.

The rest of us sure did.

❖ Jimmie Reese

Jimmie Reese was involved with professional baseball for 78 years. He joined the California Angels as a coach in 1973 at the age of 72 and remained active with the American League team well into his nineties.

Reese started as a batboy for the original Pacific Coast League Los Angeles Angels in 1917, then went on to play minor league ball in Oakland until 1929, when he was sold to the New York Yankees. Babe Ruth's roommate in 1930-31, Reese was one of many Jewish prospects the Bronx Bombers hoped to develop into a hometown hero. Jimmie was born in New York City, so playing for the Yankees fulfilled a lifelong dream. His first year in New York was a great one: he hit .336. His salary was $740.

But playing behind future Hall of Fame second baseman Tony Lazzeri stymied Jimmie's career. He was expendable and in 1932 was sold to the St. Louis Cardinals—the famed Gashouse Gang with Dizzy Dean. There he found himself stuck on the depth chart behind another future Hall of Fame second baseman, Frankie Frisch.

Because of that, Jimmie remained in the Big Leagues for only three seasons. He hit .278 in 742 at-bats.

Reese returned to the minors as a player and manager until entering the Army during World War II. After the war, he returned to minor league baseball and served as a scout, coach, and manager. He worked in seven organizations before joining the California Angels in 1973.

Jimmie was still hitting fungos to Angel outfielders while in his nineties, using a modified bat cut down the center to make it light enough, so he could swing hard enough to loft the ball to the outfielders.

Reese blamed the discord between Lou Gehrig and Babe Ruth on a conflict in lifestyles. The ultra-conservative Gehrig made no effort to befriend Ruth, who hit the town after games and rarely returned to the team hotel.

The Gashouse Gang, he often said, was a different bunch: A prejudiced group who fought, drank, and came down hard on players who didn't hustle. Fights broke out whenever a player didn't run a ball out. Jimmie said being a member of the Gashouse Gang was like being on a team comprised of 25 Pete Roses.

Jimmie Reese passed away in 1998 at the age of 97.

❖ Wally Joyner

Sweet-swinging lefty first baseman Wally Joyner made the AL All-Star team during his rookie season and finished runner-up to Jose Canseco in the voting for Rookie of the Year.

A career .289 hitter, Wally was a model of consistency at the plate, batting .280 or better 11 times in 16 seasons. He had 2,060 hits with 409 doubles, 204 homers, and 1,106 runs batted in and finished his career with a .362 on-base percentage.

Joyner was also an outstanding fielder, committing just 99 errors in 17,650 chances. He retired with a fielding percentage of .994.

Joyner made it to the postseason four times and the World Series once, losing to the Yankees in 1998 in a four-game sweep as a member of the San Diego Padres.

❖ Jack Howell

Signed as an undrafted free agent by the California Angels after playing four years at the University of Arizona, Jack was a part-time infielder and leftfielder in the Majors one year later. Although mostly a platoon and part-time player, he hit 23 homers for the Angels in 1987 and 20 more in 1989.

His 11-year career in the Major Leagues straddled a 4-year stint in Japan. He played primarily with the Yakult Swallows and briefly with the Yomiuri Giants. His experiences in Japan featured great highs but a disappointing performance in the Japanese World Series.

Howell returned to the United States in 1996, signing as a free agent with the Angels and setting a team record with four pinch-hit home runs.

A platoon player, Howell broke his wrist after joining the Houston Astros in 1998 and was forced to retire at age 37.

34

Mark Grace

A Trip to the Mound: Connors & Sutcliffe

Nobody ever enjoys watching an opposing player hit a home run, but this was doubly true in the old days at Cincinnati. Whenever one of the Reds homered, the stadium employees shot off fireworks. Not just a few fireworks but one after another—an elaborate display almost as dramatic as the Fourth of July.

When I was with the Cubs, and Rick Sutcliffe was pitching for us, on the days Rick pitched, he was cranky. In the clubhouse, on the mound, you just didn't talk to him. So one night we're in Cincy, and Sut is pitching. He gives up a home run and fireworks go off everywhere. The next hitter comes to the plate and, on the first pitch, bang! He hits a home run too. Back to back bombs. Fireworks again fill the heavens.

Our pitching coach, a guy named Billy Connors, decides to make a trip to the mound. Where Sut is very big and physically imposing, Billy is a short and heavyset. Connors climbs out of the dugout and starts heading for the mound.

Just as Connors reaches the third base foul line, Sut starts screaming at him. "Get outta here, you little bastard!" he yells. "I've got everything under control!"

Connors doesn't break stride, He keeps walking toward the mound. Despite Sut's protest, Billy hikes up the hill and joins him.

"Look, Sut," he says, "I know you've got everything under control. I'm just trying to give the guy upstairs a chance to reload the fireworks." Connors turns right back around and walks back to the dugout.

❖ Billy Connors

Billy Connors signed with the Chicago Cubs as a free agent out of Syracuse University in 1961 and had a humble playing career before going on to be a well-known Major League pitching coach and baseball executive with the New York Yankees. Billy appeared in just 26 games in three seasons with the Cubs and Mets, all but one in relief. His career record was 0-2 with a 7.53 ERA. A converted position player, Billy batted five times in the Majors Leagues. He walked twice, laid down a sacrifice bunt, and singled in two official at-bats, finishing with a .500 batting average.

His rise through the ranks of the business side of baseball began in 1971 humbly enough. He started throwing batting practice for the Mets. Billy then was a pitching coach in the minors for 8 years before advancing to the Majors for 17 seasons with the Kansas City Royals, Chicago Cubs, Seattle Mariners, and New York Yankees.

Since 1996, Connors has been a key executive in the area of player development for the New York Yankees' front office. He is based in the team's Tampa minor league headquarters.

35

Jack Howell

Hudler-san: Rex Hudler in Japan

In 1993 I was playing in Japan. Rex Hudler was a teammate, the second American over there with me while I was with the Yakult Swallows. Hud was a utility guy, kind of up and down. He didn't have much Big League time and was trying to resurrect his career.

His is a great combination of life and spirit—especially the way he plays the game with balls-out effort. Having Rex come over was good for me, because I had been there for a year, and when Hud showed up, his energy and effort gave me some life.

I had a big year, with big numbers, and was on pace in the second half to win the Central League MVP. I was close to winning the Triple Crown, too. It was huge having Rex there with me, because I was feeling a lot of pressure to keep up the pace.

In Japan, we had a lot of rainouts, even though we played on an Astroturf field. Our home ballpark was Meiji Jingu Stadium in downtown Tokyo, but whenever it rained, the team would cancel the game for whatever crazy reason; for example, if we didn't get a perfect pitching matchup, they'd postpone the game.

One night they canceled the game, but the rain subsided. The turf started to dry, so our manager called a practice; we're still going to hit and go through a two-hour workout. Hud and I are side by side, stretching on the outfield grass. The Japanese take everything very seriously, their stretching included.

Hud leans over.

"The game's been canceled," he says. "We need to lighten these guys up. Every time we joke with them, they just drop their heads. We have to do something."

We continue stretching, the humidity rises, and out come all the little bugs and worms that crawl around the turf. There were worms everywhere. I had heard a story about Rex from years past that he had eaten a bug. So I looked at him.

"Hey, Rex," I said, "I'll tell you what: If I can get these guys to put in some money, will you eat a worm?"

Rex said, "Of course I would."

I went to my interpreter, told him what I wanted to organize, and had him huddle all my Japanese teammates together. I wanted each man to put in 10,000 yen (then about $100), and we'd pool our money and get Rex to eat a worm.

Many nodded with tight smiles, but not before looking around to make sure the coaches weren't watching. The guys kicked in about $1500.

We circled Hud. I grabbed a worm and handed it to him. Rex took it, tipped his head back, stuck out his tongue, and I dropped in the worm. Rex ate it whole.

The Japanese players go nuts. One of the coaches hurries over and starts yelling and screaming in Japanese. The players put their heads down and immediately return to stretching.

Hud and the ill-fated worm really loosened everybody up. We went on to win our division and got to game seven of the Japanese Series; we nearly won the whole thing.

I like this story because it showcases Rex Hudler's personality. He loosened everyone up and brought the team closer together. The Japanese coaches are very tradition-oriented, so Rex's worm eating was something that allowed all of us to talk and have fun during the monotonous tedium of stretching.

Japanese newspapers sometimes had sketches in place of photographs. Throughout all of Japan, these sketches depicted me in full uniform standing next to Rex.

It was a big story over there. But they forgot to draw him pocketing that $1500.

❖ Rex Hudler

Hud played for the Yakult Swallows just one season, 1993, but helped the team to its second league championship in franchise history.

Few who played have loved the game more than Rex. He played 13 seasons for six teams in the Majors and played every position except pitcher and catcher.

After retiring in 1998, Hud's effervescent personality and love for the game made him a popular broadcaster for the Angels for more than a decade.

He currently resides in Tustin, California and hosts an hour-long radio show The Wonder Dog Hour. He is also president of the non-profit organization Team Up For Down Syndrome, which raises money and awareness for those living with the genetic challenge.

❖ Jack Howell

Howell had the chance to earn more money in Japan than he was making in the Majors, so he went overseas to play for several seasons. In 1992, he hit 38 homers in 113 games and batted .331. He was named Most Valuable Player, the first gaijin to win the honor in his first season in Japanese baseball.

36

Jim Abbott

Olympic Gold and Major League Red

I was on the 1988 USA Olympic team. We had guys like Tino Martinez and Robin Ventura. This was a great group of guys, and we grew incredibly close.

Looking back, it was a sweet way of playing. It was all about the gold medal. It was all about the Olympics. Having the great coaches from all over the country, like Mark Marquess from Stanford, Skip Bertman from LSU, and Ron Polk from Mississippi State.

We traveled all over. The lousy travel. Carrying your stuff everywhere for an entire summer. But it was a minor aggravation since everything that season was all about the team, and the final celebration made it all worthwhile. We beat Japan in the final game, 5-3, for the gold.

Being on the mound that day, in Seoul, South Korea, the game moving along, the idea grew that this could really happen—we could win a gold medal. After doing all the things we did, then the celebration, the screaming and yelling, and it's over.

After we'd won, and the celebration simmered down, that night we went to a casino. Charles Nagy and I were gambling. I turned 21 in Seoul. So, Charlie and I are sitting at a table, and Mark Marquess is with us. Mark is so straight-laced, it is a big shock to see him gambling with us. He is a bit conservative and takes insurance on every bet.

I'll never forget him making an order with a waiter who was barely able to speak English. Marquess looks at the waiter, then over at Charlie and me, and says, "Two beers, one Pepsi."

It was a great moment, an incredible culmination.

Contrasted with the intimacy and camaraderie of the Olympic experience, my next foray into baseball, my next level, was 1989 Major League spring training. Arriving, walking into a locker room with Major Leaguers—guys you've watched on TV all your life—going through that adjustment.

I pitched pretty well but had the feeling I was slated to go to Double A ball in the minors. Even so, there was an outside chance I could make break camp with the Major League team. A spot seemed open because starter Dan Petry was injured.

I pitched well. I struck out Canseco and then McGwire one day and made some news.

We went to Palm Springs and stayed at the Gene Autry Hotel. It was a great time of the year in the desert. While there, pitching coach Marcel Lachemann came up and delivered the news that I was breaking camp with the Major League team.

It was such a thrill. I just remember being stunned. Last summer I was in the Olympics, and now I'm going straight to the Big Leagues.

The funny part to me came after I had made the team. We travel back to Anaheim for opening day, my first professional game is in the Majors, and I'm sitting on the bench watching the rest of the guys play the Chicago White Sox. I wasn't scheduled to pitch that day but wore a Major League jersey, had all the sunflower seeds I could possibly chew, and all the bubble gum a ballplayer could ever need. And I was getting paid to wear Nikes.

Here I sit, not wanting or able to get this stupid smile off my face. This is an incredible moment for me, a kid from Flint, Michigan sitting here in sunny southern California.

The game goes on, and we start losing. We're getting beat, but I still wear that stupid smile. The game continues, and the Sox are beating us a bit worse, but it's still hard to act upset about the way the day is going. Late in the game—I don't remember the inning or score—we're getting killed, blown out at home on opening day and bring in Bobby McClure, who had about 19 years in the Big Leagues. My locker is between his and Bert Blyleven's.

McClure gives up a long home run. Next up is Ivan Calderon. Bob drills him right in the middle of the back. Calderon snatches off his batting helmet and throws it at Bob. Both benches clear.

My first day in the Big Leagues, and I'm thinking, "What in the hell?"

I'm looking around, unsure what to do. I stand up and look down the dugout to our manager Doug Rader. He's gone. He's already out at the mound, right in the middle of the fight. The melee is on.

I run onto the field, right into Carlton Fisk. He pushes me aside. Suddenly I realize I'm supposed to fight these guys.

The difference between my last amateur game and my first professional game couldn't have been more striking. Unforgettable in totally different ways.

❖ Jim Abbott

Jim was drafted out of high school but opted to attend the University of Michigan and helped the team win two Big Ten championships. He won the 1987 Golden Spikes Award as the nation's best amateur baseball player and the next year was named winner of the James E. Sullivan Award. Abbott was the first pitcher ever honored as America's top amateur athlete.

That rookie season in the Majors, Abbott won 12 games as starter. Two years later, Jim won 18 games for the Angels with a 2.89 ERA and finished third in the Cy Young balloting behind Boston's Roger Clemens and Minnesota's Scott Erickson.

Jim Abbott is one of the few to leap directly to the Majors; he never played a day in the minors.

37

Jeff Brantley

High-rolling Rook

My first trip to Veterans Stadium in Philadelphia came when I was with the San Francisco Giants, and we flew from the west coast to the east to play the Phillies. I hadn't been in the Majors for more than a month and had never been to Philly in my life. Nor had I ever heard anybody who spoke in that distinctive Philadelphia accent.

Here I am at the Vet, a pitcher still trying to sort out life in the Big Leagues, and I'm trying to figure out what I'm supposed to do as a rookie while shagging balls during batting practice. No rookie ever really knows what to do with himself at an unfamiliar stadium. But you try to figure it out on your own; you never want to be caught looking around sightseeing the stadium, because then the veterans get all over you. They will get on you hard.

This was one of those Philadelphia days where it looked like it was going to rain, but it wasn't raining. The tarp was rolled out into its outfield position, still folded but not yet spread across the field. The big metal roller they wrap the tarp around was sitting at an angle out in right field. If it did rain, the grounds crew would be able to pull the tarp over the infield very quickly. If it didn't rain, all they had to do was reposition the roller and roll the tarp back up. So, for the time being, throughout batting practice under an ominous sky, the tarp was rolled out on the field, and its big metal, cylindrical roller was parked nearby.

Norm Sherry, our pitching coach at the time, is shagging balls out in right field. Like a lot of other times, I follow him. Wherever Norm shags, I shag. Norm was 75 years old, and I follow him around to collect the baseballs off the ground, so he doesn't have to keep bending over to do it.

Because of the angle the tarp roller was positioned, the open end was facing home plate. All the ground balls heading to right field either hit the roller or bounced inside it.

Al Rosen was our General Manager, and Al was a stickler for everything. "Don't lose nothing," he'd bark. "Don't give the balls to the kids in the stands. Don't sign balls and throw them up there (into the stands). Those are our batting practice balls."

Knowing what a stickler Al was for his precious baseballs, I wasn't surprised when Norm Sherry points toward the roller and asks, "J. B., can you help me get the ball in there? I can't get in there to get it."

I crawl inside the tarp roller to retrieve the baseball. As I start trying to turn around inside the cylinder and make my way back out, the roller starts to move a little bit. Then it rolls some more. And then the roller picks up speed. It keeps rolling, and I'm trapped inside. By the time it stops, I'm all the way across the outfield in left field.

No way Norm did that himself. He may have masterminded it, but either the grounds crew or my teammates decided the rook needed to go for a ride, and you can pretty much guess the grounds crew had nothing to do with it.

I was trapped inside that thing for almost a full minute, rolling across the outfield. I got banged up so much—and so continuously—that I had bruises on parts of my body that I didn't know could bruise.

Eventually the guys mercifully stop. I fall out of the end of the thing, like a tumbling shoe stops inside a clothes dryer when time runs out. I stagger to my feet, madder than a wet hornet, and want to fight everybody, kill everybody. I'm swinging my fists wildly, trying to challenge everyone to a fight.

But I was so dizzy I couldn't see straight. Spin quickly in a tight circle four or five times and you'll get dizzy; imagine spinning in a circle from right field all the way to left field.

I finally get my bearings and equilibrium to where I can see a little bit and then get physically sick. I start to vomit. I am so sick it took nearly three hours before I could actually see straight.

I was in such bad shape that our manager, Roger Craig, made the guys come down and apologize to me—a baseball rarity since veterans don't ever apologize to rookies. I not only couldn't pitch that night, I could hardly stand up. Every time I did stand up, I got dizzy and couldn't walk.

This was an epic prank, about as bad as it gets when it comes to a group of veteran ballplayers mouse trapping a rookie. It was one of those things where you think to yourself, "You are an idiot. Here is your proof."

I was fine the next day but will never again go for a ride inside a tarp roller.

❖ Jeff Brantley

After appearing in just nine games as a tarp-rolling rookie, Brantley became a NL workhorse, appearing in 50 games or more eight straight seasons. In 1990, he was named to the All-Star team and in 1996 led the Cincinnati Reds and the National League with 44 saves.

After retiring in 2001, Brantley worked for several years as a color commentator and in-studio host with ESPN. In 2007, he left ESPN to rejoin the Reds organization as part of its well-respected broadcast team.

❖ Norm Sherry

Norm was a backup catcher for five seasons in the Major Leagues, batting just .215. But his place in baseball history is secure: while a player with the Los Angeles Dodgers, Norm was instrumental in helping fireballing left-hander Sandy Koufax transform from a wild thrower into the overpowering ace of his generation and a future Hall of Famer.

Norm toiled in the minors and the military for nine years before the Dodgers brought him up to Major Leagues at age

28. Stuck behind Johnny Roseboro on the depth chart, he got little playing time and eventually was shipped to the Mets.

Norm struggled to hit in New York, and his playing career soon ended. He quickly transitioned to coaching and worked with the Dodgers, California Angels, Montreal Expos, San Diego Padres, and eventually the San Francisco Giants. Giants manager Roger Craig was a former Dodger pitcher and teammate of Norm's back when both played in Los Angeles.

Norm managed a little less than one full season in the Major Leagues, compiling a 76-71 record for the Angels during a period that straddled the 1976-77 seasons.

38

Mark Lemke

An Infielder's Visit
to the Mound

We (the Braves) would warm up down the right field line
at the old Fulton County Stadium like we do here at Turner
Field. Every day, every single day, we're getting ready to
play the game, trying to get ourselves going, and (reliever)
Jay Howell would walk by and say, "Do me a favor. When
you go back to the dugout, you tell Bobby (Cox) don't even
think about calling down there (the bullpen) for me. Tell him
to put the phone back on the hook, forget about it, I can't
pitch today." Every day.

Well, one night Jay gets called in from the bullpen in a
close ballgame. There's nobody on, but when he finishes his
warm-up pitches, he waves for me from my spot at second
base to come join him on the mound.

As I jog toward him, I'm trying to figure out what possible scenario we'd be discussing. Signs maybe? If so, I don't
know why. There's no one on base, so I know he won't use
a different set of signals.

I get to the mound, and Jay says, "I want you to do me a
favor. I want you to turn around and tell Deion (Sanders, in
centerfield) and David (Justice, in right field) to back up."

"What?"

"Tell those two guys to back up as far as they can go."

"Why?"

"'Cause I have absolutely nothing."

"Alright, I'll do that." I turn to leave, but he stops me. I
turn and look back at him.

"Hey, hey," he says. "One other thing: you be careful out
there, too."

❖ Mark Lemke

Mark Lemke was an excellent defensive second baseman throughout his career. A small player, Lemke was a fan favorite in Atlanta and known for clutch post-season hitting on a team that made it to the World Series four times between 1991-1996 and won the Series in 1995. Mark holds of one of Major League baseball's most unusual records: In 3,664 plate appearances, he was never hit by a pitch.

❖ Jay Howell

Right-handed reliever Jay Howell pitched for seven Major League teams in his 15 seasons, going 58-53 with 155 saves and a lifetime earned run average of 3.34. Howell appeared in three All-Star games (twice with the Oakland A's and once with the Los Angeles Dodgers) and helped pitch Los Angeles to the 1988 World Series championship.

During the third game of that year's National League Championship Series against the Mets, Jay was ejected for hiding pine tar in his glove. He was suspended for the next two games.

Howell was 37 when he pitched for Atlanta, one year before retiring. He went 3-3 that season with a 2.31 ERA, giving up just 48 hits in 58 innings of work.

39

Gregg Olson

Mystery in Comiskey

❖ **Showdown: Gregg Olson versus Ozzie**
   Guillen with the game on the line

I was closing games with the Baltimore Orioles in 1992, and we were in Chicago playing the White Sox. My best pitch was a curveball. At the height of my career, it was a good one, voted the best breaking ball to come out of the bullpen in 20 years by baseball award sponsors at Rolaids, who honored the efforts of relievers.

Back when the White Sox played in old Comiskey Park, old Comiskey was famous for strange things happening. For example, a light in the scoreboard would blink when a White Sox hitter was at the plate and a fastball was coming from an opposing pitcher.

No matter what level of baseball you're playing, hitting gets a whole lot easier when you know what's coming.

New Comiskey was gaining the same reputation.

When we arrived in Chicago, we were way back in the standings for the AL East, but Chicago was duking it out with Oakland atop the standings in the West. After getting off the airport bus at the hotel, our manager Johnny Oates checked into his room. The message light was blinking on his phone. Oates picked up his phone receiver to clear the message.

It was from an unidentified source, an ominous mystery voice telling Johnny to hide his signs from the dugout and to mix up the signals from the catcher to the pitcher.

"There are," the voice said, "cameras everywhere."

The mystery caller was a male who didn't elaborate.

"Be careful," the voice said. Then the mystery voice hung up, and the message ended.

Word around baseball was that the White Sox had a legendary sign stealer on their staff, but whoever it was never sat in their dugout. He was inside the tunnel to the clubhouse or somewhere else. Whoever he was had become a famous irritant to the entire American League.

As that night's game unfolds, we take a lead into the bottom of the ninth, and Oates brings me in to close. I get two guys out, but the White Sox have a runner on first and Ozzie Guillén coming to the plate.

Ozzie always gave me trouble (as did the White Sox), so I was working hard to end the game as soon as possible. I work Ozzie quickly into a hole, a ball and two strikes. Needing one last strike to close out the game, I commenced a barrage of curveballs as wicked as I have. Ozzie could hit anybody's fastball, and I wasn't throwing one.

These yakkers snapped hard, down and in. One after the other he fouls them off. But Ozzie isn't just fouling the pitches off—he is ripping them over the visitor dugout, some up into the upper deck. He is killing them, but so far foul I keep throwing them. At some point, I'm thinking, he's got to miss. Either that or he'll get too tired to swing.

After five screaming souvenirs zoom into uncharted foul territory, manager Oates calls time out and walks slowly out to the mound. He waves the infielders and catcher to join us on the mound.

Oates looks at the catcher and says, "Don't call any more pitches."

Then he says, "Oly, put your head down and cover your mouth with your glove. Call the next two pitches right now."

I think back through the sequence of Ozzie's at-bat, bow my head, and talk to the palm of my glove.

"Curveball," I say, "and then a high fastball."

Nobody says a word. We split up, the guys go back to their positions, and Oates goes back to the dugout. I'm alone on the mound, wondering what the hell is going on. One minute,

I'm immersed in a mano en mano end-game battle, the next minute I'm a secret agent, playing some sort of spy game. Whisper, the room is bugged.

I glance around behind me. The infield is ready, I pretend to take a sign, and come set.

Uh-oh. I throw a pumpkin-sized curveball right down the heart of the plate, easily the most hittable pitch I've thrown. Ozzie freezes. He just stands there, bat on his shoulder, following it with his eyes all the way into the catcher's glove. Strike three called. Without a word of protest, he pivots back to the dugout.

Game over. Somewhere The Voice is smiling.

❖ Ozzie Guillén

Ozzie Guillén is a former shortstop who played 16 seasons for four teams before going on to become the first Latin-born manager to win a World Series. In 1985, Guillén was the AL Rookie of the Year with the White Sox, where he was also a three-time All-Star. He won a Gold Glove in 1990. Guillén ranks among the White Sox all-time leaders in games played (1,743), hits (1,608), and at-bats (6,067). He won the National League Pennant in 1999 in his only full season with the Atlanta Braves but lost the World Series to the New York Yankees. Ozzie won the World Series in 2005 as the manager of the Chicago White when his team swept the Houston Astros in four games.

❖ Johnny Oates

Johnny Oates played catcher for six teams in 12 Major League seasons (1970-1981): the Chicago White Sox, Baltimore Orioles, Atlanta Braves, Philadelphia Phillies, Los Angeles Dodgers, and New York Yankees.

Oates began managing in the minors in 1982, the year after he retired as a player, and won the Southern League title with the New York Yankees' Double-A Nashville Sounds.

In 1988, Oates rejoined the organization that originally drafted him, the Baltimore Orioles, and managed their Rochester AAA affiliate. The following season he was promoted to the Majors as first base coach under Frank Robinson. After Robinson started 13-24 in 1991, Robinson was let go, and Oates was named manager.

In his first two full seasons with the team, Oates led the Orioles winning records and won The Sporting News Manager of the Year Award, but after the strike-shortened 1994 season, the team's new owner, Peter Angelos, dismissed him.

Oates was quickly hired by the Texas Rangers, who had just fired Kevin Kennedy. He led the Rangers to their first playoff appearance in team history and shared the AL Manager of the Year Award with the Yankees' Joe Torre.

Oates continued to lead the Rangers for several more seasons and won AL West titles in 1998 and 1999. After a mediocre 2000 season and bad start to 2001, Oates resigned and was replaced by third base coach Jerry Narron.

After a break, Oates was considering a return to managing but couldn't. He was diagnosed with an aggressive brain tumor and died on Christmas Eve, 2004 at age 58 at Virginia Commonwealth University Medical Center in Richmond.

40

Brian Giles

Down on the Farm
with Billy Rip

The 1994 season was stopped because of the players' strike. Because of it, when we go to spring training in '95, we've got a mere three weeks to get ready. This is my first year on the 40-man roster, and I know I have no chance to get to the Big Leagues. As expected, I am optioned to the minors, to AAA Buffalo.

Because of the strike and what was going on in baseball—guys getting blackballed, the attempted salary cap that the owners wanted and didn't get—a lot of guys who should have been in the Big Leagues instead are playing in Buffalo, New York. Among them were Billy Ripken, Todd Frohwirth, Gregg Olson, Casey Candaele—a bunch of guys. None of them deserved to be in the minor leagues; but because of the salary structure and the circumstances in baseball after we reached the labor agreement, they were.

I'll never forget Billy Ripken. First of all, he was so fed up—he couldn't believe he was in the minor leagues—he decided to make a yearbook about his 1995 minor league season with Buffalo. Two of the photographs I remember vividly. One Billy took in Nashville, a photograph of the spread on the table. Two fly-stick streamers are dangling down from the ceiling right over the food, both stuck full of eyes and wings and the body cavities of a ton of dead flies.

Billy's other picture came from one of those minor league flight itineraries where we get up at four in the morning to get to the airport in order to fly to the city we were playing in later that day. I think we were going to Indianapolis, which was the absolute worst for getting our luggage.

We land and go wait for our luggage to come spitting out of the baggage claim carousel. I will never forget the sight of Casey Candaele crawling down through the baggage claim conveyor belt, disappearing out of sight. We hear the echoes of him down there yelling at the baggage handlers on the truck, imploring them to deliver our stuff.

He's down there yelling, when all of a sudden the conveyor belt cranks up. Here comes Casey, riding up and out on a suitcase. An emperor's arrival if ever I saw one.

Those were two of my favorite memories. Funny what a guy remembers after a life in baseball, isn't it? It's not always the Big League stuff. Sometimes it's the guys you play with who you remember more than the cheering and the hits.

The good thing about that year for me, even though some of those guys got screwed, was that it was a good learning experience. I got to the Majors for the first time that year after a September call-up.

The Major Leagues are awesome. But with the right bunch of guys, any year can be your most fun year in baseball.

❖ Brian Giles

Once Brian got called up to the Majors, he stayed there. He played 15 years, getting 1,897 hits with a .291 lifetime average. A very disciplined hitter, Giles walked 1,183 times, five times walking 100 times or more in a season. A left-handed outfielder, Brian made two All-Star teams and five times received league votes for MVP. Six times a .300 hitter, Giles hit over .300 three straight seasons for the Pittsburgh Pirates.

Although he reached the postseason five times, Giles lost his only World Series, the 1997 fall classic where his Cleveland Indians were beaten by the Florida Marlins in five games.

❖ Bill Ripken

A hardworking overachiever, Bill broke into the Major Leagues in 1987 and played with his brother and father, Cal Jr. and Cal Sr., on his hometown Baltimore Orioles. He played parts of a dozen seasons, but that 1995 post-strike season in Buffalo was the toughest. After five years as a starter and eight years in the Majors, he was recalled to play just eight games that season. Bill responded by going 8-for-17 at the plate.

A lifetime .247 hitter, Bill had neither the size nor physical skills of his Hall of Fame brother, but he played the game hard, and he played the game right. Despite his limited playing time, Bill once led the American League in sacrifice hits and another time was third. In 1992, he led AL second basemen in fielding percentage (.993) and two other years finished in the top five.

41

Gregg Olson

Fans Go Postal: Even the Mailman's A Suspect

During my career with the Orioles, I lived in a house in rural Reisterstown, Maryland. My home was north of the city and a pretty easy commute to the ballpark. Our community was an established, well-treed area. It was really nice.

Baltimore is a great city and a great place to play. It has a small town feel that is great to live in. But sometimes for a player, anonymity is better than celebrity. A ballplayer in a slump can hide in New York or Chicago. He cannot hide in Reisterstown.

Looking back on my time with the Orioles, it's safe to say I loved everything about playing in Baltimore—except when I didn't pitch well.

Since everyone knew where Cal Ripken Jr. lived, and I lived near him, some of the fans figured out where I lived, too. If I could have eliminated just a few of those people, life would have been fine.

I came to the Major Leagues with Baltimore and got off to a fast start. I was American League Rookie of the Year in 1989 and had another consistent year in 1990. But in 1991, for the first time I struggled. I don't think I was throwing that badly, I just wasn't getting a whole lot of love—nothing bounced my way. Consequently, automatic saves became exciting saves, and exciting saves turned into blown saves. Fan loyalty in the world of a relief specialist is a bit fickle. Some love you know matter what. Others decide based on the scoreboard.

As things turned out, someone who didn't like blown saves figured out where I lived. Every time I blew a save, I lost a mailbox. I ended up blowing eight. During the game, I'm pitching my best. After the game, I'm wondering if there's a sale at Home Depot.

My wife and I had made the move to Reisterstown at the end of the 1990 season, once it looked like the club and I were a good fit, and we could anchor down. She thought it would be nice to buy a birdhouse mailbox. She bought a large, wooden, house-looking thing and happily had it installed.

First blown save of the year, I come out the following morning and find scattered kindling in a 50-yard circle where my mailbox used to be. My neighbor's mailbox, still held together by a rubber band, is fine. It is untouched.

"All right," I'm thinking, "no problem. I'll piece most of it back together until I can pick up a new one."

Funny thing was I thought the birdhouse demolition was a random accident.

Next blown save, the mailbox is gone. Not blown up. It's gone. Disappeared without a trace.

"Okay," I decide, "let's get a cheaper one, maybe they'll lose interest." Third blown save, and my new, cheaper mailbox is stolen too.

If I weren't screwing up Major League baseball games, this would be amusing. After losing three of four mailboxes, Cal and Kelly Ripken bought us a housewarming gift: an indestructible mailbox. This was a very kind gesture that eliminated them as suspects.

The mailbox's installations directions said to anchor the massive mailbox post in cement. If I did, the directions promised, nothing could go wrong. What the directions forgot to point out was that if and when I blew another save, an enterprising and motivated baseball fan could chainsaw the post in half.

❖ Gregg Olson

When Gregg left the Orioles after arm troubles sabotaged his 1993 season, Gregg's need to plant and replant of variety of mailboxes suddenly ceased. After bouncing around through both leagues for the next several seasons but getting a chance to close again for the fledgling Arizona Diamondbacks, he signed a two-year free agent deal with the Dodgers that proved to be the last of his career.

Gregg and his family decided to move and traded Reisterstown, Maryland for a new home at an enclave in southern California that's populated with many former, retired players.

Now an advance scout for the Padres, Gregg is also the president of Toolshed athletic sportswear. Toolshed fans are loyal but not emotional; Olson happily retrieves the bills and occasional fan mail in peace.

<h1 align="center">42</h1>

<h1 align="center">Gregg Olson</h1>

<h1 align="center">Call to the Pen: Todd Frohwirth Answers</h1>

We are at home in Baltimore, and Todd has just come to us from Rochester, our AAA affiliate. Todd has pitched in the Big Leagues before, with Philadelphia the year before, and came to the Orioles as a free agent. A right-handed reliever, he had been in Rochester for 20 games or so before being called up.

The custom in the bullpen is for the pitching coach to do a pre-call to the bullpen. The pre-call is a quick discussion between the pitching and the bullpen coaches, since the pitching coach wants to know how a reliever feels before suggesting him to the manager.

A pre-call usually goes something like, "Ask how (name of reliever here) feels." The reliever in question responds with his status.

The first day Todd is in the bullpen with the Orioles, the pre-call comes in the fifth inning. Elrod Hendricks, our bullpen coach, takes the call. He looks at Froh and says, "Todd, they want to know how you feel."

To which Frohwirth responds, "Tell them I have a little bit of a head cold, but thanks for asking."

❖ Todd Frohwirth

Todd pitched exclusively in relief, appearing in 284 games in nine seasons with Philadelphia, Baltimore, Boston, and California. Primarily a setup man, he pitched with a low, submarine-style delivery and finished his career with a 20-19 record and 11 saves. Todd finished 92 games, 53 during his last two seasons with the Orioles. He appeared in 65 games in 1992 and 70 more (6th most in the American League) a year later.

After that, he was never the same. He returned to AAA and pitched for four teams. He retired after short trials with the Red Sox and Angels and is currently a Major League scout.

43

Brooks Robinson

Bob, Earl, Emmett, & Pat

❖ All About Bob

I signed out of high school in 1955 when I was 18 years old. The first club I have to report to is in York, Pennsylvania. I get to York one day earlier than expected, and the ballclub had very little information on me.

I go into my first game around the sixth inning, put in for defense at second base. The announcer is a guy named George Trout, who is still a friend of mine. The only information George has been given about me is that my name is B. Robinson.

George figures my first name had to be Bill or Bob or something like that. So he turns on the PA system and takes a guess.

"Now playing second base for the York White Roses, Bob Robinson."

Welcome to pro ball, Brooksie. My very first game as a professional, and I get introduced under an assumed name.

* * *

❖ A Mound Chat with Earl Weaver

All game long our manager, Earl Weaver, has been hollering at the umpire about balls and strikes. Earl finally calls time out, walks slowly out to the mound, and plans to take out his pitcher.

When Earl arrives on the mound, he just stands there. He doesn't motion toward the bullpen or engage either the pitcher or catcher in discussion. He just stands there.

The home plate umpire gets impatient and wants to know what Earl is going to do. Tired of waiting, the ump walks out to the mound to go find out. When he reaches the mound, he walks up to join the conversation.

The umpire asks, "What do you want, Earl, the left-hander or the right-hander?"

Earl replies, "Guess."

"What?"

"That's right, guess. You've been guessing all night, so guess which one I want."

The umpire threw him out of the game, one of 97 times Earl Weaver got tossed.

* * *

❖ Earl Weaver and Umpire Emmett Ashford

Emmett Ashford was the first black umpire in the Major Leagues. He was a very diplomatic man with a good sense of humor, one of the few in blue who could get along with Earl Weaver because Emmett knew how to handle him.

One day we're playing, and there's a bang-bang play at first base. Emmett is umpiring, and the throw beats our guy. Emmett calls the runner out.

Here comes Weaver, shot out of the dugout like a cannon-ball. Earl runs all the way out to first, screaming the entire time. "How can you call that guy out? He beat the play!"

Well, Emmett looks at Earl and says, "Earl, let me tell you something. He touched the base with the wrong foot."

Befuddled, Earl turns and walks toward the dugout. He suddenly stops and turns around.

"Emmett," he says, "don't you know that the runner can touch the base with either foot?"

The batter remained out.

* * *

❖ Earl Weaver and Outfielder Pat Kelly

One thing that drove Oriole manager Earl Weaver crazy was a player swinging at pitches out of the strike zone. He wanted hitters with discipline. Whenever a guy expanded the zone by making a bad decision and taking a hack, Earl went berserk.

So, here we are at home in Baltimore hosting the Minnesota Twins. It's the bottom of the ninth, two out, the bases are loaded, and Pat Kelly is up. With a walk we win, a base hit we win. Win and go home.

Full count to Pat Kelly, and the pitch comes in. It's high and well out of the strike zone. He swings and misses. Strike three: third out, side retired, inning over, game still tied. Instead of a W, we have to go back out and keep playing.

Weaver is livid. He runs over and rants at Kelly.

"How can you swing at that ball? If you don't swing, we go home, we win! How can you swing at a ball over your head, you can't do that!"

The game plows on. Finally, the 13th inning rolls around. The game is still tied, and Weaver is still fuming. Earl looks down the bench and spies Kelly down at the end. He calls out, "Pat, you know we would be home having a cocktail or eating dinner right now if you hadn't swung at the ball out of the strike zone."

Pat, an ordained minister, has his fill of Weaver's sputtering. He rises off the bench, walks down to Earl, puts his arm around his old manager's shoulder, and says, "Earl, have you ever thought about walking with the Lord?"

Earl Weaver is someone who always gets the last word, quick with the quip. "Kelly," he snaps, "have you ever thought about walking with the bases loaded?"

* * *

❖ About Brooks Robinson

It didn't take long for every baseball fan in America to call Brooks Robinson by his first name. An anchor at third base for 23 seasons with the Baltimore Orioles, Brooks won 16 consecutive Gold Gloves and earned the nickname "The Human Vacuum Cleaner." From 1960-1974 he made 15 straight All-Star teams.

Brooks' stay in York was short, and the PA announcer quickly learned who he was, as did the fans. Brooks hit .331 with 11 homers in 95 games and, still just 18, was promoted to the Orioles for a six-game taste of the Majors. He went 2-for-22 and spent the next season in the minors to gain experience.

By the age of 22, Brooks was a full-time, every day Major League third baseman. He went on to have a magnificent career, winning virtually ever honor available. He was the AL MVP in 1964, the All-Star MVP in 1966, the World Series MVP in 1970 after an electrifying performer against Cincinnati with both his bat and glove, and was voted into the Hall of Fame the first year he was eligible.

❖ Earl Weaver

Short, fiery, volatile, animated, and intense, chain-smoking Hall of Fame Manager Earl Weaver managed the Orioles to a winning tradition for 17 seasons.

Born and raised in St. Louis, Weaver played minor league ball for several seasons but was a good-fielding, weak-hitting second baseman who never got close to making the Majors. Earl quit playing to become an independent team manager at 26 and then joined the Oriole organization the following year.

Weaver managed his way up through the minors, reaching AA in 1962 and AAA in 1966. He won three championships in 11½ minor league seasons and was a consistent winner. Throughout his minor league journey, Earl won 55 percent of his games.

Earl Weaver became manager of the Orioles midway through the 1968 regular season and in 17 years would have just one losing season. Weaver led Baltimore teams to six Division titles, four AL pennants, and the 1970 World Series championship. For his Major League career, Earl was 1,480-1,060—an outstanding 58.3 percent win ratio. Five times his teams won 100 games or more during the regular season, three times in a row from 1969-1971.

Notorious for his battles with umpire Ron Luciano and others, Weaver was ejected from 97 games and caused a forfeit in another. He pulled his team off the field in Toronto in protest because bricks held down a bullpen tarp, and Weaver argued his leftfielder could be injured. Umpire Marty Springstead refused to do anything about it, so Weaver pulled his players off the field. Springstead forfeited the game to the Blue Jays.

Weaver used stats, his bench, and platoons long before they became popular and eschewed "small ball" in exchange for the big inning. Good strategy involved, in his words, "Double-plays and the 3-run homer." He also pioneered the use of radar guns in spring training and, as an aside, became well known for growing tomatoes inside the ballpark at Memorial Stadium.

In 1996, the Veterans Committee voted Earl into the Baseball Hall of Fame.

❖ Emmett Ashford

Emmett was the first African-American umpire in baseball, calling American League games from 1966-1970. His second year in the Majors, Emmett worked Anaheim's 1967 All-Star Game as an outfield umpire.

Emmett Ashford broke color barriers in the minors too and reached the Majors late—he was 51 when he called his first Big League game. Since baseball had a mandatory retirement age of 56, Emmett was forced to stop working after the five-game 1970 Orioles—Reds World Series. Had the Series extended to six games instead of ending with the Orioles winning in five, Emmett would have been behind the plate for game six.

A stylish dresser and flamboyant with his on-field gestures, Emmett was a sometimes polarizing official. Some folks loved him because of his style while others thought it excessive.

Born and raised in Los Angeles, Emmett died of a heart attack in 1980 at age 65 in Venice, a nearby Los Angeles suburb.

❖ Pat Kelly

Signed by the Minnesota Twins out of Simon Gratz High School in Philadelphia, left-handed outfielder Pat Kelly spent 15 seasons in the Major Leagues, four with the Baltimore Orioles. He was on the 1973 AL All-Star team while with the Chicago White Sox and finished that season hitting .280. Fast with limited power, Kelly stole 250 bases, including 40 and 34 his first two seasons in the Majors. Pat normally had a very good eye at the plate; he walked 588 times—once every eight trips to the plate.

Pat played in one postseason, homering and driving in four runs to help Baltimore beat the Angels and advance to the 1979 World Series against Pittsburgh. The Orioles lost to the Pirates in seven games. Pat went 1-for-4 with a walk in five plate appearances.

Pat Kelly, a reverend for Lifeline Ministries in Maryland, died from a heart attack October 2, 2005 at the age of 61.

44

Robin Ventura

The Clubbie Trade

The Chicago White Sox and the Baltimore Orioles have two clubhouse workers who are beloved by all who play there. Newt works for Chicago, and Butch works for the O's.

The Orioles were visiting us in Chicago one year when someone got the inspired idea to trade the two clubbies. We got our head of media relations to issue a press release that stated Harold was traded to the Orioles for Butch. It was a straight-up deal, man for man. Everyone is in on it. We packed all their stuff and shipped them—and their gear—to the opposite clubhouse.

Butch comes over to join us, tears in his eyes. He doesn't want any part of the deal because he is a diehard Orioles fan. He can't believe the team has traded him.

Newt goes over to the Baltimore side. Davey Johnson (the Orioles' manager) speaks with him. Newt is very upset about the trade. He thinks he is a 10/5 guy. With 10 years of Major League service, five with the same team, a player cannot be traded without his consent. Newt thinks the rule should apply to clubhouse workers, too. He thinks he should not be traded.

When we break the news the trade is just a prank, both guys fly back to their clubhouses faster than peregrine falcons.

No one is above a good Major League prank. And I mean no one.

❖ Robin Ventura

A 16-year veteran of Major League baseball, Robin won six Gold Gloves at third base and was a two-time All-Star. Robin's first 10 seasons were spent with the White Sox, who drafted him 10th overall in the first round of the 1988 draft. He then played three seasons for the New York Mets, two for the Yankees, and finished as a part-time player for two seasons with the Los Angeles Dodgers.

A .267 lifetime hitter, Robin hit a career best .301 in 1999 for the New York Mets along with personal highs for home runs (32) and runs batted in (120). A solid player, Ventura finished with 294 home runs and 1,182 runs batted in.

Robin played in eight series during five visits to the post-season and made it to the World Series in 2000, when his Mets were defeated in five games by their cross-city rivals, the New York Yankees.

45

Tony Clark

Don't Mess with Dad

During spring training of 1996, I am on the Detroit Tigers, and we are out on the field doing our morning stretching. Our strength coach is Brad Anders, and Brad is a guy who respects his players.

During this particular stretch, he groups us by tenure. Everybody with 15-plus years runs, then everybody with 10-15 years runs, and so on. When the 10-15 group runs, Cecil (Fielder) is in the group. From somewhere down the line, somebody makes the comment that time in Japan doesn't count.

Needless to say, the boys who heard this player say that distance themselves. The comment eventually echoes its way to Dad (Cecil). He doesn't say a whole lot about it then, but you can tell it bothers him—the disrespect agitates him quite a bit.

After stretching, we get to hit, so we all walk over from the stretch field toward the batting cage. Well, Dad doesn't come right into the cage. Everybody else is in the cage, hitting and getting loose.

All of a sudden, Dad shows up pushing a wheelbarrow. In the wheelbarrow are this particular player's (the bigmouth's) clothes. Dad's arrival stops everything going on in the cage. He asks everyone to please pay attention to what's in the wheelbarrow.

He explains, "If anyone else has any smart aleck comments that they want to make, in reference to his accomplishments and his time in the Big Leagues, all they need do is speak up now.

"For the gentleman who spoke up earlier, this is what is going to happen to him and anybody else who shares that similar point of view."

Dad takes lighter fluid, squeezes the can, and sprays it on the pile of clothes in the wheelbarrow. He lights the clothes on fire.

As we watch, us young guys are in awe. A player's clothes just got burned up, just for making a comment. As we look around, the older vets on the team have that "We told you so" look on their faces.

To this day, I don't know if Cecil bought clothes for that player or gave him money to buy some. Maybe he simply had a point to make and made the guy suck it up—I still have no idea.

What I do know is that a young ballplayer with less than a year in at the time threw a respect grenade for the value of time served (in baseball) and showed a lack of respect to those who have served it. And in the event that a player wishes to throw in his two cents with respect to someone who has logged the time and put in the hours and put up the numbers, perhaps this should be the end result. You want to disrespect a veteran? Fine, become one first.

What Cecil did that day is something that still resonates with me today, so many years later. I tell this same story to young guys in spring training who decide they want to be a little more vocal. Perhaps they should, not that it would be followed through like Dad chose to do. Times were different back in the day. If this was said, then this is what would happen. It is something I will never forget.

Here I am, way more than a decade later, still talking about the day Cecil swirls on the lighter fluid and smokes the man's threads. Good clothes are hard to find. No sense getting them torched during BP for opening your mouth when it should've stayed closed.

Seems a lot smarter to wait your turn, stay quiet, and take your rips. And put in your time.

❖ Tony Clark

The second overall pick in the 1990 draft by the Detroit Tigers, towering (6'8") switch-hitter Tony Clark played 15 seasons in the Major Leagues and was a 2001 All-Star. A .262 hitter with 251 career home runs, Tony twice made the postseason (with the Yankees in 2004 and the 2007 Arizona Diamondbacks) but lost both times during the League Championship Series.

Tony got off to one of the fastest starts in Major League history, slugging 50 career home runs in his first 202 at-bats, which spanned two seasons. He finished third in the voting for the 1996 AL Rookie of the year behind Yankee shortstop Derek Jeter and White Sox pitcher James Baldwin.

An outstanding all-around athlete, Tony played college basketball at the University of Arizona and San Diego State, where he led the team in scoring.

❖ Cecil Fielder

Long before his son, Prince Fielder, was hitting long home runs into the seats and hitting 50 homers in a season, Cecil was. A thick, powerfully built right-handed slugger, Cecil (pronounced Sess-il) played 13 years in the Majors. He hit 319 home runs and drove in 1,008. Cecil led the American League in runs batted in three successive seasons with 132, 133, and 124. He also led the league with 51 homers in 1990 and 44 the year after. Every full season of his career, he hit more homers than doubles and triples combined.

Cecil hit some prodigious shots in his career and was one of four men to hit the ball over the left-field roof at Tiger Stadium (Harmon Killebrew, Frank Howard, and Mark McGwire were the others). He is the only man ever to blast a baseball completely out of Milwaukee County Stadium. Lefty Dan Plesac of the Milwaukee Brewers was the man who threw the pitch.

Cecil only spent one season in Japan—1989—and was wildly popular over there because of his tremendous power. He slugged 38 homers for the Hanshin Tigers, who lured him over with a salary eight times greater than what he was making with the Toronto Blue Jays. His big year and immense popularity increased Fielder's desirability back in the United States, and he returned to the Majors the following season with Detroit. He slugged 51 homers that season and established himself as a full-time force in Major League Baseball.

46

Mike Scott

Itch Powder: the Great Equalizer

A lot of useful things fit in a baseball player's locker. Among my favorite while with the Mets was itching powder. We got some, and it was really nasty stuff. All you had to do was put it on the tip of your finger and touch someone. Once it's on a person's skin, he or she will start itching and can't stop.

I was with the New York Mets for my first four seasons before going to Houston in 1983. Early in my career with the Mets, we used the powder on one of our catchers, John Stearns. Stearns was a good guy, but his nickname was "Bad Dude." He acted like he was a bad dude, but he really wasn't. Bad Dude was just his image.

We dust John in the clubhouse, and it takes a little while before the powder does its job. We clear out of the clubhouse and get on the team bus. Stearns doesn't know why, but suddenly he's itching and scratching.

One of the guys lets John in on the joke, that somebody got him with itching powder.

Still scratching, Bad Dude stands up, looks around the bus, and threatens, "If I find out who did this, we're going to Fist City."

Nobody's a Bad Dude when he's been nailed with good itching powder.

❖ John Stearns

Stearns was a fast, hardnosed catcher—a collision player who played aggressively for a bad team and was a fan favorite because of it. A football star at the University of Colorado,

Stearns was drafted into the NFL by the Buffalo Bills but chose to play baseball instead. Stearns was the second pick in the 1973 draft, taken by the Philadelphia Phillies after the Texas Rangers selected high school pitching phenom David Clyde. Taken immediately after Stearns were future Hall of Famers Robin Yount from a California high school and Dave Winfield out of the University of Minnesota.

Bad Dude batted .260 for his career and was extremely fast for a catcher. He often hit second for the Mets and finished his 11-year career with nearly twice as many stolen bases (91) as home runs (46). Persistently hampered by injuries, Stearns only had three seasons where he played as many as 100 games. Despite that, he made the NL All-Star team four times; but each of those years, his Mets lost nearly 100 games.

John played all but one of his 810 career games with the Mets. He appeared in his first Major League game with the team that drafted him, the Phillies, but suited up just once. He went 1-for-2, but a three-for-three trade during the winter sent him to the Mets and left-handed reliever Tug McGraw to Philadelphia.

Stearns has stayed in baseball as a scout, coach, and minor league manager.

47

Doug DeCinces

Playing Catch with a 12-Year-Old

I can share this now, but at the time, it frightened the bee-jeezus out of me. Back in the summer of 1972, I was playing minor league ball in Asheville, North Carolina for Cal Ripken Sr. Senior was our manager, and Cal Jr. would come down and stay with us for the rest of the summer after he got out of school in Aberdeen, Maryland where the Ripkens lived. Even as a kid, Junior was dedicated. He took ground balls with me every day. He was 12 years old.

Sunday games in the minors were day games, and one Sunday both infield practice and batting practice were rained out. The thunderstorm finally blew through, and the rain stopped. As soon as it cleared a bit, Cal Jr. grabbed his glove, stood next to me in front of the dugout, and the two of us began playing catch with another guy.

The ballpark in Asheville had a short porch in right field, and behind the fence, a hill climbed directly up 100 feet. Houses were side by side along the ridgeline and overlooked the field. I throw a ball to Cal and all of as sudden hear "BANG!" An object whizzes by me, and the grass in front explodes.

I know exactly what it is: it's a gunshot.

I am in the Air National Guard Reserve at the time, have gone through training, and instantly realize what's going on. Oh my gosh, someone is shooting at us! Another "BANG!" The second bullet blows up the ground five feet in front of me. I grab little Cal Jr., by the back of his uniform and dive with him into the dugout. Twenty feet to safety, and he never touched the ground.

It didn't take long for the police to solve the case. A 15-year-old kid just released from juvenile hall is shooting at us from his house on the hill overlooking right field. After the police assure us there will be no more assassination attempts, they give us the "all clear" to go ahead and play the game.

The whole time we're out there playing, I'm aware that I've got a large number on my back and am playing second base 100 feet closer to the houses overlooking right field. I'm thinking, "Now I'm in range. I'm going to hear another shot." There were no more shots, that night or any other night.

Ten years later, I am traded from Baltimore along with Jeff Schneider to the California Angels for outfielder Dan Ford, so the Orioles could make room for their new, 6'4" slugging third baseman: Cal Ripken Jr.

48

Doug DeCinces

Thurman, Billy & Me

Back when I was with the Baltimore Orioles, we were home for a game against the New York Yankees. Earl Weaver is our manager, Billy Martin theirs. Both teams are in heated competition for the division title.

I had good success against the Yankees in our previous series in New York. My luck continues in our first game back home in Baltimore. I hit a home run.

When I step into the box for my first at-bat in the series' second game, Yankee catcher Thurman Munson says, "Billy (Martin) wants to know what pitch you want to hit."

I step out of the box and look at Thurman.

"C'mon," I say, "don't be doing this stuff. What are you doing?"

"No, seriously. You tell us what pitch you want to hit because every pitch I call, you hit."

In the heat of a pennant race, I don't trust either one of those guys, Billy or Thurman. "Thurman," I say, "let's just play the game."

Well, the umpire is watching us and listening. He starts laughing. I don't appreciate that so I test him, asking, "You guys think this is funny?"

"No, no," the umpire replies, nodding toward the Yankee dugout. "Look over at Billy."

So I look over and Billy (Martin) is standing on the top step with his hands in the air, waving that it's okay. Whatever pitch you want, DeCinces. Go ahead. Pick it.

As I dutifully step back into the box, I'm trying to keep my composure and think through all this stuff. Like I said, I don't trust them. I'm going to call a breaking ball, and I'm

184

going to get a fastball in the ear. I have no confidence in what's about to happen, so Thurman gives me some help.

I dig in, and Thurman says, "I'm going to tell you what's coming. The first pitch will be a fastball." Sure enough, fastball. I don't swing, and it's a strike. I step back and steal a glance toward the Yankee dugout. Everybody in it is laughing.

Hmmm, it's Christmas. It's legit. "Okay," I tell Thurman, "fastball."

Fastball comes in, ball one. "Okay," I say, "slider."

Ron Davis is pitching, and he throws really hard. Davis has two very good pitches, his fastball and slider. I've seen the fastball twice, so now I'm just kind of testing. Davis misses with slider, ball two.

I like the fastball better and want another one. "Okay," I say, "fastball."

Davis throws me the heater, and I pop it up. I dutifully run it out, all the way down the first base line. I can hear Billy Martin howling, the entire Yankee dugout laughing. I get back to our dugout, and Earl Weaver asks, "What the heck is going on? What is Billy saying to you?"

Those two guys (Billy and Earl) would always go at each other, all the time. In any way possible, one would try to get an advantage over the other. I tell Earl what happened.

He looks at me and says, "Why didn't you just hit the pitch?"

I just look at him, wanting to explain that it's not that easy.

Earl said, "The next time you go up there, you call a pitch you want, and you hit it."

So, my head's really crowded when I come to the plate for my next at-bat. Thurman greets me and asks what pitch I want this time.

"Fastball." I foul it straight back. Without waiting for him to ask, I call for another one and dig in deep, ready to rip.

"Okay," I say, "fastball." Foul this one straight back, too. Two fastballs and I'm in the hole 0-2. Nuts. I'll get the next one. "Another fastball." Ball one.

"Okay, slider."

Davis winds up, throws the slider, hangs it out over the plate, and I hit a home run over the wall in right-center. Hit it really good.

I come up again later in the game and tell Munson I want another fastball.

Thurman looks at me, yanks down his catcher's mask, and drops into his crouch. Gruffly he snorts, "Billy said that game is over."

❖ Doug DeCinces

Doug hit plenty more home runs during his 15-year career, finishing with 237. After nine seasons with Baltimore, DeCinces hit a career high 30 homers and drove in 97 runs while hitting .301 in his first year with the California Angels. He finished third in the AL MVP voting that year and won a Silver Slugger. A third baseman, Doug made the All-Star team the following year. He played in one World Series with the Orioles, losing in seven games to the 1979 Pittsburgh Pirates.

❖ Thurman Munson

Yankee captain and catcher Thurman Munson played 11 seasons for the team that drafted him fourth in the first round of the 1968 amateur draft, going from his college campus at Kent State to Yankee Stadium in one year. He is the only Yankee to win the Rookie of the Year (1970) and the American League's Most Valuable Player (1976).

Munson hit .300 with 100 runs batted in three straight years and got six consecutive hits during the 1976 World Series. Thurman was a member of seven All-Star teams, six in a row, and won three Gold Gloves. In 1976, he was named the first Yankees team captain since Lou Gehrig retired in 1939.

Thurman Munson died on August 2, 1979 when his private plane crashed at Canton, Ohio during a flying lesson on one of the team's few days off. He was 32.

❖ Billy Martin

Fiery infielder Billy Martin played 1,021 games in 11 years in the Major Leagues and made the 1956 AL All-Star team. A mediocre hitter during the regular season, Billy was a different player in the postseason, hitting .333 in five World Series with the Yankees, four of which the team won. In the 1953 Series the Yankees beat the Brooklyn Dodgers in six games for their fifth straight title—an all-time record. Billy went 12-for-24 with five runs scored and eight driven in and won the Series MVP.

Martin was traded six times in his career and retired after being released in 1962. Seven years later, he was back in the Majors as manager of the Minnesota Twins. He managed for five organizations (the Yankees multiple times) and was 1,253-1,013 over 16 seasons. He managed the Yankees to the 1977 World Series title. Billy's last season was 1988, when he was 40-28 before owner George Steinbrenner replaced him with Lou Piniella.

Billy was a passenger in a friend's pickup truck and died in a car crash near Binghamton, New York on Christmas Day, 1989. He was 61.

49

Doug Flynn

Closing In On Pete

I wasn't drafted out of high school, so I went to college at nearby University of Kentucky. There I got kicked off the baseball team because I wasn't good enough, or so I was told. I wanted to prove the coach wrong, so I kept trying, and eventually the hard work paid off. I became a pro player. But my career began the hard way; I signed out of a tryout camp, a cattle call for guys like me who dreamed of playing pro baseball.

A few years later, I made it the Major Leagues as a utility infielder for the Cincinnati Reds. I grew up in Lexington, 80 miles from Cincinnati, so the Reds were my hometown team. I grew up a huge Reds fan and rarely missed a game on TV. To be on the Big League roster of my favorite team at the age of 23 was a thrill in itself. I made the team in 1975 when the Reds were a baseball powerhouse.

The first game of the season, manager Sparky Anderson puts me in to bunt a runner over. The next night I'm starting at shortstop because Dave Concepcion is hurt. My first at-bat that night, I make an out. My second time up, I get a base hit. I'm fired up. I'm on base thinking, "I got a hit in the Big Leagues, and my parents are here to see it!"

The inning ends with me stranded on second. I look over and see Pete Rose coming out of the dugout bringing my hat and glove. I can't believe it. Pete Rose bringing my stuff! I know standing there that I will remember this moment for the rest of my life. Here is a living legend who is going to be the all-time hits leader, and after my first Big League hit, he's bringing out my hat and glove.

Pete trots over to within two feet from me, throws my stuff into my stomach, and says, "Here, kid. You're only about 2500 (hits) behind me."

❖ Doug Flynn

Doug played 11 seasons in the Majors and went on to get 917 more hits. But Pete Rose was right—Doug finished way more than 2,500 hits behind him. A modest hitter with little power, Flynn was known as an excellent fielder and won a Gold Glove in 1980 while playing second base for the New York Mets. Although Doug didn't hit for a high average (.238 lifetime), he was tough to strike out. He fanned just 320 times in 4,085 plate appearances.

❖ Pete Rose

Pete played for 24 seasons, participating in more games (3,562) than anyone else. In addition to his all-time hits record (4,256), Pete went to the plate more often—15,861 times—than any man in history. He batted .303 for his career.

The 1963 NL Rookie of the Year, Pete Rose entered baseball hustling, and some say he's never stopped. A 17-time All-Star, Pete was the NL MVP in 1973, won two Gold Gloves, and one Silver Slugger. Rose scored 2,165 runs during his career and is first on the all-time list for singles (3,215) and second in doubles (746). Only Tris Speaker, with 792, hit more.

But for all Pete's accomplishments on the field, it's his off the field problems that keep storm clouds hovering over his legacy. As he nears his seventieth birthday, Pete signs autographs for money in Las Vegas.

50

Mike Cameron

Nice Boxers, Lou

I was playing for Seattle, maybe 2001 or 2002, sitting in the clubhouse along with Edgar Martinez, Bret Boone, and a couple of other guys, Arthur Rhodes I think, and maybe Bob Boone, Bret's dad. We're talking about hitting. It's Saturday night, and we have a day game on Sunday.

We had been struggling a bit. Lou (Piniella) was still managing the club and had the whole place smoked up with cigarettes. Eventually he comes out of his office to join us wearing only his boxers, which were all stretched out with holes in them. Lou has no shirt on, no shoes. He is scratching his head and rubbing his belly while he's talking about hitting. We've all had a few beers by this time, a few cigars, and we've been anchored down in the clubhouse since the game ended hours before.

Lou loves to talk about hitting and must have gone on about hitting for about two hours, sitting there in his holey boxers. You can imagine what he looks like when he stands up to demonstrate, trying to teach hitting principles wearing only those ratty undershorts and moves in slow motion.

Visualize it: "You get into your stance . . ."

Come on Lou, I felt like saying, go put a shirt on, something. But I don't say a word. He's there, doing his thing.

I think we all finally called it quits and went home around three in the morning, I don't know if it was that late, but it was pretty late considering we had a day game the next day. It was way past midnight, way past.

I arrive at the ballpark the next day, and Lou has never left. He's just stayed the night in the clubhouse. When I walk in, he's wearing the same shorts and heading toward the shower.

I ask him, "Lou, did you go home?"
"Nah, didn't make it home."
"You gotta be kidding me."
That night is one of my favorite baseball stories. All of us just sitting there, no one in a hurry to leave, talking baseball for like three hours. I'm sure I've had other days like that, but this one was really special. Sitting in the company I was in. Bob Boone played 19 years, Lou played 18. Edgar played 18, too. He averaged .312. And here we all stayed, way past midnight, still talking baseball.

Things like that that don't go on now, nobody does that anymore. Now you go some places and you can't even get a beer. For the obvious reasons, you know, but I guess I can say I got a chance to come up in a really good era of baseball, the nineties, the mid-nineties as a matter of fact. To be able to have youth experiences like what I saw then is something that always sticks with me. Those memories carry me through the ruts even as the years roll by, and I continue to play today. It's the guys, as much as the game, which makes baseball such a perfect sport.

❖ Mike Cameron

Mike paid attention that night to what Lou was talking about in his underwear. On May 2, 2002, Cameron hit four home runs in the first five innings of a game at Comiskey Park. Fourteen men have homered four times on one game. No one has ever hit five.

An 18th round draft choice by the White Sox in 1991 out of LaGrange High School in rural west-central Georgia, Cameron made it to the Majors at 22 and has gone on to become an All-Star centerfielder and three-time Gold Glove winner. A free-swinger at the plate, Mike strikes out about once a game, but when he hits, he hits with power. In 16 seasons, he hit 278 Major League homers and drove in nearly 1,000 runs.

Although Mike made it to the postseason four times—twice with Seattle and once with San Diego and Milwaukee—he never made it to the World Series.

He would never be caught dead in underwear similar to Lou Piniella.

51

Gregg Olson

A Piping Hot
New York Pizza

It was 1988, the Orioles were headed for 107 losses, and when September rolled around, and the rosters were allowed to expand, most of the organization's minor league stars were called up to the big club in Baltimore. My phone rang, too. I was lucky enough to receive my first call to the Major Leagues.

We only had a month left to play, but I joined the team in time for a road series in New York against the Yankees. I had never been to Yankee Stadium and was excited just to be there.

They've flip-flopped the bullpens since, but back then the visiting team's pen was on the centerfield side. Yankee Stadium also featured tiered bullpens, with each bench row higher than the one in front, sort of like stadium seating in a movie theater.

Elrod Hendricks, our bullpen coach, sat on the lower level near the bullpen telephone. The rest of us sat up top, a row behind him. During the fourth inning, catcher Terry Kennedy snuck out to a door in centerfield, opened it, and disappeared. When he walked back 10 minutes later, out of sight of the fans and coaches, he was carrying two boxes of hot pizza.

Terry sat on the bullpen bench, opened a box, reached in, pulled out a slice, and started eating. Along with all the other relievers, I joined in. At the time, my pro baseball experience consisted of eight weeks in the minor leagues. How did I know eating pizza in the bullpen of a Major League game at Yankee Stadium was frowned upon? I was just enjoying the evening: Yankee Stadium, in uniform, a hostile September Bronx crowd, hot pizza, a great seat. Best of all, I was getting paid. Beat the heck out of studying biology at Auburn.

Yep, I enjoyed it all, right up until the eighth inning when Elrod got up to answer the bullpen telephone.

"Olson," he called, "you're in the game."

"Oh good," I said, "I get to play. Who do I face?"

"Rickey Henderson, Dave Winfield, and Jack Clark."

Welcome to the Big Leagues, son.

Needless to say, on the long stroll in I felt like a box of rocks. I remember walking up onto the mound for my Yankee Stadium debut, fabled Yankee announcer Bob Sheppard announcing my name. I also remember holding my glove close to my chest as I accepted the ball from my manager, legendary Hall of Famer Frank Robinson.

Frank did not need to see pizza sauce.

❖ Terry Kennedy

The sixth selection in the 1977 draft out of Florida State, Kennedy played 16 seasons in the Major Leagues, two with Baltimore. A four-time All-Star, the left-handed hitting catcher's best season was 1984 with the San Diego Padres. He hit .284 with 17 homers and 98 runs batted in and was given a Silver Slugger Award for being the best offensive catcher in the National League.

Terry twice made it to the World Series, once with the Padres and once with the San Francisco Giants. He homered in game four of the 1980 series, but the Padres lost to Detroit in five. In 1989, Kennedy's Giants were swept in an earthquake-delayed four games by their Bay area neighbors, the Oakland A's.

❖ Elrod Hendricks

A native of St. Thomas in the Virgin Islands, popular Oriole player and coach Elrod Hendricks joined the organization in 1968, nine years after signing his first pro contract as an amateur free agent with the Milwaukee Braves.

Most of Elrod's 12-year Major League playing career was as a part-time catcher, but his first few seasons he helped the Orioles to the greatest run of success the franchise has ever had. For three straight seasons, 1969-71, Elrod's outstanding defensive skills and work with the pitching staff helped the Orioles reach the World Series.

While losing to the Miracle Mets in 1969, the next fall Elrod hit .364 with a home run and four runs batted in when the Orioles beat Cincinnati's Big Red Machine. In 1971, the Orioles lost in seven games to the surging Pittsburgh Pirates' "We Are Family" club, led by Hall of Famer Willie Stargell. Elrod also played in the 1976 World Series while a member the New York Yankees, losing in four straight to the Cincinnati Reds.

Near the end of his career, Elrod returned to the Orioles and, at the age of 37, manager Earl Weaver put him in a game to pitch. Elrod pitched shutout ball, retiring seven of the nine men he faced, giving up a lone single and one walk.

After his playing career ended, Elrod became Baltimore's bullpen coach, a position he held for a team-record 28 seasons. A mild stroke forced Elrod out of uniform in 2005. He died that winter, one day shy of his 65th birthday.

52

Goose Gossage

There's Nothing
Like Support

When I joined the Yankees in '78 as a free agent after one season in Pittsburgh, I put a whole lot of pressure on myself. I came over in the off-season thinking I'd team with Sparky Lyle as the best righty-lefty bullpen combination ever.

But it didn't work out that way. They (the Yankees) handed me Sparky's job on a silver platter. Sparky had won the Cy Young award in 1977 as the American League's best pitcher. Despite that, they made me the closer. Combining the pressure of being new and pitching in New York didn't help. I started the season struggling and continued to struggle for several months.

Back then in Yankee Stadium, whenever a reliever was called into the game, he got a ride in from the outfield bullpen in a blue-and-white pinstriped Toyota. Since I wasn't doing well, when the phone rang for Gossage, the instant the fans saw me reach for the Toyota door, they started booing. They booed me to death. I was hoping for more support at our home opener but didn't get it. When I was introduced, they booed the hell out of me.

I couldn't blame them. I lost games every way conceivable. We had opened on the road, and when we returned home, I was 0-3.

During this stretch of bad outings at home in Yankee Stadium, driving me in from the bullpen created a unique set of challenges for the Toyota driver. I was the only guy on the staff that necessitated driving with the windshield wipers on, since everything the fans had in their hands and could throw was pelted down upon us. You name it, the Yankee fans threw it: beer, soda, hot dogs, popcorn, and popcorn boxes—they fired everything they had.

Back then it felt a little lonely out there on that mound. It didn't help when I bent over, picked up the resin bag, and turned to face my catcher, Thurman Munson.

He would look at me and say, "Well, how you gonna lose this one?"

The first time he said it, I couldn't believe it. I said, "I don't know. Why don't you get your little ass back there, and we'll find out?"

One time I was brought into the game to face a big jam, either bases loaded or men on second and third. I step on the rubber, look in to the catcher, and search for his sign. Munson is nowhere close to giving a sign. He's squatting behind the dish laughing.

I immediately step off to compose myself. I step back on the rubber and look back in. Thurman is still in his crouch and still laughing. I step off again, angry now that he doesn't seem to have any sense of urgency to get out of this mess and end the ballgame.

It happens again, a third time. Finally, Thurman turns to the ump, calls time, and trudges out to the mound. I'm fuming. As soon as he reaches my dirt circle, I bark, "What the hell is so funny?"

He answers, "Check Rivers out." Mickey Rivers is my center fielder, so I turn around and look. In deep center, he's posed in a deep sprinter's crouch, fingers in place along the imaginary starting line, his butt propped up and waiting for the starter's pistol to go off. Mick the Quick is in position and ready to go, ready to run down my mistakes.

I have to laugh. It is hilarious.

❖ Rich "Goose" Gossage

A flamethrower for 22 seasons, Hall of Fame relief pitcher Goose Gossage went 124-106 with 310 saves during a career in which he appeared in 1,002 games and averaged nearly two innings per appearance. Gossage was tough to hit and even tougher to take deep. He gave up an average of just 7.4 hits per nine innings and surrendered only 119 homers to 7,507 Major League hitters.

Goose pitched in three World Series, winning a game and the series in 1978 when the Yankees beat the Dodgers. He pitched in eight World Series games, going 1-0 with a 2.63 ERA.

Gossage made nine All-Star teams during an 11-year span and five times received MVP votes despite being a closer. Rich retired following the 1994 season and returned home to Colorado. He was the only player selected to the Baseball Hall of Fame in 2008, his ninth year of eligibility.

53

Goose Gossage

Mickey Rivers, Hood Ornament

Right after I start pitching for the Yankees, I'm in a stretch of bad months, and every time I make a move, I'm booed. Yankee fans are great to winners but unforgiving to losers. I was blowing games left and right, and they watched my every move. When I'm all warmed up and ready to go and climb inside the passenger seat of the relief pitchers' pinstriped Toyota, I'm physically and mentally ready to enter the game. The Toyota is warmed up too. It's Danny the groundskeeper's job to drive me in.

All of a sudden, Mickey Rivers comes running all the way over from centerfield and sprawls across the hood of the car.

"Oh, please, Danny," he pleads, "don't bring him in. We want to win this game. Please don't bring him in." Mick refuses to move, spread across the car hood for a good five minutes.

The delay aggravates the umpires. I'm looking over top of Rivers, whose face is flush against the windshield. I can see the umpires frantically waving to Danny to drive the car toward the mound.

Well, Danny doesn't want to move, because Mickey is on the hood. The fans love it; 55,000 people are laughing.

Finally, the second base umpire runs from his infield position all the way out to the bullpen. When he finally arrives, he is huffin' and puffin.' He marches up to Rivers, who's still on the hood, and asks, "What in the hell is going on out here?"

Rivers looks at the umpire. "We don't want Goose to come in," Mickey says. "We want to win this game."

199

This causes the umpire to start laughing, too. "Mickey," he says, "you have to get off this car. You're holding up the game."

Mick finally relents. He slides off the hood and runs back out to his position in centerfield. He gets a thunderous ovation every step of the way.

All Rivers was trying to do is what (Thurman) Munson used to do—try to get me to relax and have some fun out there. I was tight, and they knew it. They also knew I'd never pitch my best unless I relaxed and calmed down.

That season ended up being an amazing one for the team and our fans. We were 14 games out in August and ended up catching the Red Sox on the last day, forcing a one-game, winner-moves-on playoff at Fenway Park.

I ended up pitching the last 2 2/3 innings of that playoff game, and we won. Then we beat the Kansas City Royals in the AL playoffs and the Dodgers in the World Series. We were able to repeat as world champions.

To commemorate our late-season success, on the inside of our World Series rings, Mr. Steinbrenner had the jewelers engrave the words, "the greatest comeback in history."

That's one way to look at it. Another might be that it wouldn't have been the greatest comeback in history if I hadn't dug us such a deep hole to begin with.

❖ Mickey Rivers

Mick the Quick played 15 seasons in the American League and made the most of his three full years with the Yankees: He won three pennants and two World Series. Happy-go-lucky and fast on his feet, Mickey batted leadoff and played centerfield. He hit .295 for his career and batted .300 or better seven times. He also is one of the few players with more triples (71) than homers (61). He was an excellent base runner, stealing 267 bases during his career and leading the American League with 70 in 1975 while with the California Angels. He and Ed Figueroa were traded to New York for

Bobby Bonds during that off-season, and Mickey made the All-Star team his first season in New York. He finished third in MVP balloting behind teammate Thurman Munson and Kansas City's George Brett.

Rivers was always good for a quote. For example, here are some pearls we've borrowed from his website, MickeyRivers.com:

"Me and George and Billy are two of a kind." Mickey on his relationship with George Steinbrenner and Billy Martin

"Out of what, a thousand?" Mickey responding to teammate Reggie Jackson's claim he has an IQ of 160

"Pitching is 80% of the game and the other half is hitting and fielding." Mickey breaks down the success keys to winning baseball

"No wonder you're all mixed up. You got a white man's first name, a Spanish man's second name, and a black man's third name." Mickey to Reginald Martinez Jackson in July 1977

"I'm going to double my limit." Mickey's response to a 1975 interview question asking how many bases he's going to steal that season

"He's so ugly. When you walked by him, your pants wrinkle. He made fly balls curve foul." Mickey on former Major Leaguer Danny Napoleon's looks

"He is so ugly he should have to wear an oxygen mask." Mickey on teammate Cliff Johnson's looks

"I might have to commute. You know, left field, DH, wherever." Mickey on where he'll be playing

"The first thing you do when you get out to center field is put up your finger and check the wind-chill factor." Mickey on defensive positioning

"The wind was blowin' about 100 degrees." Mickey's response to a question about the wind at Chicago's Comiskey Park

"I felt alone out there, like I was on a desert island. I felt like Gilligan." Mickey after playing left field for the first time

"I like playing on this team. We actually been doin' real good. Got a different mix here. Most important thing is you gotta keep pickin' up in paces. That's why we're playing contentious play. We got top names, guys can still hit in the majors, guys been out of the game hittin' the ball, shockin' it. Don't have no old, old guys. Not sayin' they don't get a good job done. Fact is, they've been vice versa. So that's incentive right there. It's been a plus." Mickey analyzing his team in the 1989 Senior Professional Baseball League

"That felt good. I hadn't hit off a lefty in two months." Mickey's post-game comment after doubling off Boston Red Sox right-hander Bob Stanley

"I threw about 90 percent fastballs and sliders, 50 percent fastballs and 50 percent sliders. I'm starting to sound like Mickey Rivers." John Butcher, former Texas Rangers pitcher

Not all of Mickey's observations dealt with baseball. For example:

- *"What was the name of that dog on Rin Tin Tin?"*
- *"I didn't want the wind to hit me, so I tried to outrun the wind."*
- *"It was so cold today that I saw a dog chasing a cat, and the dog was walking."*

Born and raised in Miami, Mickey still lives in South Florida. He owns and operates the Mickey Rivers Baseball Academy in Pembroke Pines, a suburb of Fort Lauderdale.

54

Jeff Brantley

Game Three of the Earthquake Series

❖ October 17, 1989

I remember getting ready for game three of the 1989 World Series. I was a rookie. It's bad enough being a rookie—but being a rookie in the World Series is much worse. We were now home at Candlestick Park after losing the two ballgames across the bay to the Oakland A's.

We're inside of our locker room and in order to get from our locker room to the home team's first base dugout, we have to go underneath the stadium through a 50-yard tunnel. When we leave the locker room, we walk down a few steps to a flat walkway where we hit the stairs that lead to the dugout.

Being the third game of the World Series, this is our introduction day at Candlestick. Things are crazy, with everyone hustling around, screaming to hurry up, checking to make sure we're wearing the right uniform. Everything is chaos.

My biggest concern is just trying to figure out which shirt to put on. I want to make sure I am dressed correctly. My personal life is hectic, too. My wife and I have a little girl, my parents are in town, and mother-in-law is babysitting our baby daughter at our apartment.

Finally dressed and ready to go, I exit the locker room door and walk down the hallway toward our dugout, as giddy as I can be. Ten steps down the tunnel corridor, I feel something and hear something that seems like a train. The rumbling grows louder and louder and louder.

It hits me: EARTHQUAKE!

I don't want this; I'm beneath the stadium. I'm under five million tons of concrete and steel. But this is how a pitcher instinctively protects his arm: I grab my glove and shove it under my right arm and begin to run.

The lights go out; so much for emergency lighting at Candlestick. Here I am stuck in this dark tunnel, and all I can see is a faint, distant light way ahead of me—our dugout.

I put my hand on the concrete wall and run through the darkness, stumbling over too many things to count. I'm fumbling, stumbling, and losing my balance. It's everything I can do to reach the dugout and fresh air.

I am not breathing well. Nothing is falling on me. I'm having a panic attack.

I finally reach the dugout, my glove beneath my right arm, and now I'm searching the stands for my wife. I spot her and wave her down onto the field.

Everyone, it seems, is looking at me, everyone asking if I'm alright. Over and over, the same question, "Are you alright?"

I'm not even thinking about it. "Yeh," I say, "I'm fine."

Over and over, the echo of others: "Are you okay?"

"Yes, I'm fine, I'm fine. Where's my wife?"

I'm hunting for my wife, wanting her by my side. Same with my mom and dad. This is their first trip to California. They're from Alabama and have no idea about earthquakes. They are safe, out in the parking lot, away from the stadium. I locate my wife, and she joins me on the field.

By now all the players are moving toward second base because earthquakes always arrive with a secondary problem—aftershocks. The aftershock is the worst, that's when things fall. The earthquake breaks and loosens things. The aftershock for a 7.0 earthquake is usually about 5.0, as it was with this. That's when everything falls. My wife and I are out by second base, waiting for the aftershock, and I look down at my hands.

Sliding a finger across raw concrete feels like rubbing it across sliced metal. That's what happened to my hand, and that's why everyone kept asking what was wrong with me. When I had put my left hand on the wall for stability and ran down through the tunnel hallway, the mortar and rough bricks ripped my hand apart.

I have blood all over my uniform and don't think a thing about it. It never crosses my mind that I am bleeding until everything has settled down, and I notice it. The blood is why everyone keeps asking if I am okay.

The game is canceled. My wife and I find my parents. It takes 6½ hours to get to the car and start driving back to our apartment in San Mateo. There is no cell service, and we cannot call from the ballpark. We have no inkling at this point that the Bay Bridge has collapsed, as has the 880 on the Oakland side.

No one knows who's dead, who's alive, or what area is devastated most. Everything is a guess, other than a report that there are fires in the Marina district.

The drive is a terrified crawl. My wife is praying. Anybody who's mothered or fathered a child knows the gut-wrenching fear that explodes in your mind if you're uncertain your boy or girl is alive or dead. That's all she's doing, praying and praying and praying some more that our baby and her mother are okay. It will take us 4½ hours to drive what normally takes 30 minutes.

What happened? We still don't know. Everything we keep hearing is across from San Mateo in an area of Foster City called Landfill. Radio reports gossip that everything is sinking back into the bay because that area is unstable, reclaimed land. Is it true? We don't know. We just creep along.

We fear our daughter has drowned in quicksand; that's what is going through our heads. My wife prays even harder.

We see tremendous damage on the way up to our apartment complex. The brand new luxury hotel my mom and dad are staying in, I think it was a Hyatt, is condemned.

We finally arrive where my mother-in-law and daughter are. Emily, our little girl, is not quite two years old. She's outside running around on the grass. Emily has no awareness of the disaster, but my mother-in-law is not so immune. She is psycho-babbling. A southern lady from Clinton, Mississippi, she is terrified. She's never been through anything like this. None of the rest of us has either.

Everything inside the house that was facing north to south rolled with the wave of the earthquake. Everything facing east to west fell over and crashed.

I'll never forget my dad saying, "You know, son, I was up on the balcony facing toward the south bay as the earthquake came up. It looked like a wave people could surf on.

"The water looked like a big tidal wave. But when it (the quake) hit the ground at the parking lot at Candlestick Point (almost 1½ miles from the stadium), the ground started rolling like the wave.

"All the cars that were parked facing north and south, they just rode the wave. Every car that was facing east and west skipped a space. That's why all the alarms were going off in the parking lot, because they hit each other."

The San Francisco earthquake was one of those things you look back on and think, "I sure am blessed to make it through that and be able to tell a story about it."

Whether you play baseball or watch it, cherish your family and the life you're living. They are what matter most.

❖ The Earthquake World Series

The 1989 World Series was won in a four-game sweep by the Oakland A's but took more than two weeks to play. The earthquake, later named the Loma Prieta quake, disrupted the series for 10 days. With much of the city severely damaged by the earthquake, San Francisco's Giants fared little better. In four games, the team was outscored 32-14 and never had a lead. Because of the postponements, Oakland only needed two starting pitchers—Dave Stewart and Mike Moore—to win all four games of the Series.

The Giants had won the division by three games over San Diego and then beat the Cubs for the NL championship in five games. The A's cruised past Kansas City in the division and then took out Toronto in five games to earn its way to the Series.

Like Jeff Brantley, umpire Al Clark was getting ready in the locker room when the quake hit at 5:04 p.m., 11 minutes before game time. Clark never finished dressing. When the tremors hit, he ran out onto the field in his underwear.

❖ Jeff Brantley

A sixth round draft choice in 1985 out of Mississippi State, Brantley pitched for five ballclubs in a 14-year career. He was a reliable short relief workhorse, appearing in 50 games or more during eight straight seasons. A 1990 All-Star with the Giants, in 1996 Jeff led the Cincinnati Reds and the National League with 44 saves and won the Rolaids Relief Award as the league's best relief pitcher.

Brantley pitched in 11 postseason games and posted a career 2.40 ERA.

After retiring at the age of 37, Brantley spent several years as a TV personality with ESPN before leaving the cable network to rejoin the Cincinnati Reds organization. He remains a popular part of the ballclub's highly respected broadcast team.

55

Gregg Olson

Sweet Revenge: Drowning Billy the Marlin

In 1994, I was a reliever with the Atlanta Braves, and we were on the road in South Florida, in town for a series against the Florida Marlins.

The first night, as was his nightly custom, their mascot—Billy the Marlin—rides around the stadium and circles the stands during the seventh-inning stretch. He sits up on the back of an open convertible, his Marlinmobile.

The other pitchers and I are sitting down the left field line on the bench and in folding chairs in the visitors' bullpen. We're model citizens, minding our own business, as Billy and his driver approach.

Suddenly Billy the Marlin reaches down, pulls out a high-powered water gun, and hoses down our bullpen. Nails us, big-time. The crowd roars with laughter as Billy rides triumphantly back to whatever aquarium he snorkels in between games.

What Billy did not know is that Major League pitchers do one thing extremely well: they adjust. And adjust we did.

Just as a good pitcher always prepares for competing during the game, our bullpen geared up for the next night's seventh-inning stretch. Fool us once, Mr. Fish, and shame on you. Fool us twice, shame on us.

The next afternoon I tour Fort Lauderdale with a buddy, stockpiling an arsenal comprised of every type of water-launching device the clever people of China have ever mass produced. For insurance, we grabbed a couple bags of water balloons, the round kind easiest to throw. My pal drops me off at the ballpark early, so I have time to distribute the goods.

All of us destined for the bullpen that night load up ahead of time, filling the water guns and water balloons. We go so far as to cart out a bucket of water hidden beneath a towel, so we can refill the squirt guns. Billy is a predictable foe; we know when he will arrive, from which direction, when he'll come into range, and how far we can reach before he'll be out of range. As he no doubt is nibbling pre-game sushi, we prepare a counter-assault.

Our relievers gather around for a brief meeting to strategize the battle plan. There are six of us: Steve Bedrosian, Mike Bielecki, Mike Stanton, Greg McMichael, Mark Wohlers, and me. The plan is to fan out, with certain guys assigned certain seats. We have folding chairs, so we design the most efficient trap possible, especially since Stanton and McMichael are southpaws. Wohlers could throw 100 miles an hour, so he is hidden behind the net protecting the stands. Bedrosian and I crouch behind the waist-high wall that separates foul territory from the bullpen. There Bedrock and I are safely hidden from sight.

When the seventh inning arrives and Billy the Marlin's chariot rides by in seeming triumph, he pulls out his little peashooter of a squirt gun to spray our bullpen.

We're ready, waiting, and spring into action. The air is instantly alive with powerful water cannons, a barrage of water balloons, and hurled buckets of water.

We execute with near-perfect military precision. We drown that stuffed fish before he is halfway past. The coup de gras comes when Wohlers pops out from behind the screen and nails Billy the Marlin with a 90 mile-per-hour water balloon head shot. Wohlers' balloon impacted with such accurate velocity that it nearly spun the fish's beak completely around his shoulders. I turn and call out congratulations to Wohlers. He's been having control trouble lately.

For some reason Steve Bedrosian decides to go off-script and empty an entire water bucket inside Billy's passing convertible. As we rise in unison from behind the wall, Bedrock whirls and hurls the contents of the bucket toward the car. I am in the middle and have turned to nod to Wohlers. I never see it coming. Bedrock drills me in the back, with only scattered raindrops escaping to sprinkle Billy's driver.

There I stand, drenched and dripping, a casualty of friendly fire. Billy never got me—my own guy did.

Nothing's easy at the Big League level, not even revenge on a mascot.

❖ Billy the Marlin

Eight feet tall and 250 pounds, Billy the Marlin was named by original Florida Marlins owner Wayne Huizenga and first appeared February 25, 1993. For the team's first decade, the man inside the billfish suit was John Routh, a clever and talented performer who had previously developed the character Sebastian the Ibis into a nationally known mascot for the University of Miami.

Routh and the Marlins parted ways after 10 years, largely for cost-cutting reasons. Routh was inside the suit the night the Braves unloaded on Billy. He survived that night and continued to wage war on all visiting ball clubs. Although replaced by others who've worn the Marlin suit since, none have approached the popularity of Routh's original Billy.

❖ Gregg Olson

Olson masterminded and orchestrated the Braves' Billy the Marlin hit with help from co-author Ocean Palmer. Palmer scooped up Olson at the team hotel in Fort Lauderdale, went on a toy store bombing run, and delivered the reliever—arms laden with bags of water guns, balloons, and attack paraphernalia—right to the players' entrance at the ballpark.

After drenching Billy, the Braves relievers handed all their empty water guns up and over the railing to a nearby group of young cheering fans.

56

Will Clark

Canseco's Lucky Shoes

I was playing in Texas with the Rangers, and, at the time, Jose Canseco was going through one of those 0-for-30 spells that lurk in the mind shadows of every Big Leaguer who's ever held a bat.

At the time Canseco insisted on wearing a pair of lucky spikes that had holes in them. To put it kindly, these things were shot; they were more than worn out—they were on their final mile.

Well, a few of the guys decide it would be a great idea to go ahead and burn Jose's shoes in the clubhouse. I guess we considered it a ritual sacrifice, since torching a guy's cleats is not a common occurrence.

We pour alcohol all over Jose's shoes, spark a flame to life, and light them. They burst into flames. As they burn, we rain dance around them.

Jose is out on the field and gets wind of what's going on. He comes running into the clubhouse, sees his shoes in flames, and screams in panic. "Hey!" he pleads. "Wait, wait, wait! Those are my lucky shoes!"

I look at him in disbelief. "Lucky shoes? You're for 0-for-30 in these shoes."

We finish the burning, Jose gets a new pair of cleats, and that very night he hits three home runs. If his old shoes were lucky, these new ones were a whole lot luckier.

❖ Will Clark

A six-time All-Star and four time top-five vote-getter for Most Valuable Player, lefty first baseman Will Clark's sweet swing produced a lifetime .303 batting average and 2,167 hits, 1,186 runs scored, and 1,205 runs batted in during a remarkably consistent 15-year career. Ten times Will batted .300 or better for the season and he averaged more than one hit per game throughout his career. He won two NL Silver Sluggers for offensive excellence and one Gold Glove (1991) for defense.

Will Clark reached the postseason five times with three teams, losing as a member of the Giants in his only World Series, beaten by Canseco's Oakland team in 1989. But he was electrifying while lifting his club past the Cubs to get there, going 13-for-20 (.650) with six extra base hits (two home runs) and eight runs batted to help power the Giants to the NL pennant.

❖ Jose Canseco

Born in Cuba, Jose and his baseball-playing brother Ozzie were brought as infants to the United States and raised in Miami. Word of his prodigious power and tape measure home runs spread quickly through the minor leagues; when called up to the Oakland A's late in 1985, Canseco hit five homers in 29 games and began an exciting and controversial 17-season American League career.

In 1988 Canseco became baseball's first "40-40" man, hitting a league leading 42 home runs and stealing 40 bases. He drove in an AL best 124 runs that season and was voted the league's Most Valuable Player.

By time he was finished, Jose Canseco hit 462 homers and drove in 1,407 runs. He was the 1986 AL Rookie of the Year and a six-time All-Star. Canseco played in four World Series and won two—with the A's in 1989 and the Yankees in 2000. Although he hit three homers, Canseco batted just .152 in 14 World Series games.

Whether he was doing something good or something bad—or just in the wrong place at the wrong time—Canseco was fun to watch. On August 31, 1992, he was traded in the middle of a game while in the on-deck circle. The next season, in a Ranger game against the Cleveland Indians, Carlos Martínez hit a fly ball that Canseco lost sight of as he drifted across the warning track. The ball hit Canseco on the head and bounced over the wall for a home run.

Three days later Canseco asked his manager, Kevin Kennedy, to let him pitch the eighth inning during a blowout loss to the Boston Red Sox. Kennedy relented and Canseco gave up three runs in one inning and ruined his arm, requiring Tommy John reconstructive elbow surgery.

Life after baseball for Canseco has been difficult. After earning an estimated $45 million in salary during his playing days, his homes have been repossessed, and his services are available for hire for things ranging from spending a day with him to celebrity "fighting."

Baseball's most visible and controversial mouthpiece to the broad-based steroid scandal he helped nurture, Canseco has been arrested multiple times for events ranging from spousal abuse to bar brawls to drug smuggling across the Mexican border.

57

Jim Palmer

Pitch Counts & Earl's Pearls

One of baseball's biggest current discussion points is pitch count. I was hurt when Earl (Weaver) took over as manager of the Baltimore Orioles at the All-Star break in 1968 but was ready at the start of the 1969 season. My teammate, Mike Cuellar, would go on that season to win the Cy Young Award, sharing it with Detroit's Denny McLain.

Cuellar's first start of the year is against the Minnesota Twins. The Twins have (Cesar) Tovar, a great leadoff guy, (Rod) Carew, who won seven batting titles, (Tony) Oliva with three batting titles, and (Harmon) Killebrew with 500-plus home runs.

The game heads into the ninth inning; I'm keeping the pitch chart because I'm starting the next day. We are winning 5-2, Mike has thrown 133 pitches going into the ninth, and Tovar is due to lead off.

This is the first time I have kept a chart for Earl. As the inning begins, Tovar reaches, so I walk down to the end of the bench and say, "Mr. Weaver, that's his 135th pitch."

Earl snaps, "Why don't you get your ass down to the end of the bench? I'll let you know when he's tired."

I return to the far end of the bench and resume keeping the chart. Carew is the next hitter, and he hits into a double-play. Oliva flies out to centerfield, and the game is over. Mike ends with 142 pitches and a complete game win.

After going out to congratulate Mike and my teammates, I return to the dugout. Earl is waiting. I duck my head down and try to get into the dugout, but he stops me and says, "Now do you know how I feel about pitch counts?"

If you couldn't make good pitches, Earl would take you out. In the old days, if you were pitching well, they left you in. When you were pitching bad, they took you out. That was Earl's theory, how he managed the game. Cuellar threw 290 innings that year. He won 23 games and completed 18 of 39 starts.

* * *

❖ Earl's pearls: a slow start at Fenway

One of my favorite stories happened when I was pitching with a hurt shoulder against the Red Sox in Fenway. My previous start was against the Yankees in New York, and I pitched a one-hitter throwing about 80 miles-per-hour. I got a cortisone shot on a Monday at home in Baltimore, we go up to New York, and I pitch on Wednesday. I was so slow Elston Howard was swinging before the ball even got there. Horace Clarke hits a single up the middle in the seventh inning; he's the only guy to get on. Jake Gibbs hits a double play ball, Clarke's erased, and I face the minimum 27 guys.

My next start is in Fenway Park, and my arm is killing me. The first hitter is Mike Andrews, and he hits the game's first pitch for a double off the wall. George Scott hits the second pitch of the game like a rocket into left. He hits it so hard that Andrews can't score. Don Demeter hits the third pitch into the screen above the Green Monster. I've thrown three pitches and given up a double, single, homer, and three runs.

Earl doesn't want to come talk to me. He knows I'm only throwing 80, so he sends our pitching coach, George Bamberger, out to the mound. Bamby was a great guy and doesn't even look at me when he gets to the mound. Instead, he looks at Andy Etchebarren, my catcher.

"Etch," he asks, "how's he throwing?"

I'll never forget this: Andy replies, "How would I know? I haven't caught one yet."

❖ Negative positive

Earl believed in the "negative positive." He thought that if he gave you enough negatives, the cumulative effect would turn out positive.

For example, you have a one-run lead, pitching in Fenway Park, and Yaz, Rice, and Fisk are due up. All three are home run hitters. You tell yourself to be aggressive and not to walk anybody. As your foot is on the top step of the dugout and you're ready to head out there to face them, you hear this little echo: "Can't get beat until you walk somebody." This was Earl's idea of being positive.

Rich Dauer came up to the Major Leagues out of USC and used to hit into a lot of double plays. Earl used to tell Richie, "Pop up once in a while, save us an out." Again, that was Earl's way of being positive.

❖ Spring training

Earl always held meetings near the end of spring training. They were productive because we always had winning teams—we'd win between 90 and 109 games. In that respect—winning—Earl was great to play for. During these final spring training meetings, he'd say, "Listen, I'm taking the best 25 guys in the organization. If we play as one and we do things the Oriole way, we're going to have some success."

One year, about 95 games into the season, we've lost 50 and won just 45. We have a good team but haven't really gelled. Once the regular season began, Earl called very few meetings. So if he called one, you sat on your stool in front of your locker and faced the center of the room. Earl calls us together, so we gather around.

Earl stands in the middle of the locker room and says, "I made a mistake." Earl never admitted that he made a mistake, so now we're all leaning forward.

"Yeh," he says, "I picked the wrong 25 guys."

❖ Sliders

Earl was Earl. Dave McNally was a 20-game winner for us four times. McNally, Cuellar, and I are in the dugout—three of our four 20-game winners since Pat Dobson hasn't come out of the clubhouse yet—and we're getting ready for early hitting. Weaver comes over to give us a lecture on pitching.

He looks at McNally and says, "You have to use your slider." Earl never played higher than AA ball, the reason being that he couldn't hit a slider. He drove in 102 runs in A ball but when he got to double A, they started throwing the slider. That's why the slider was Earl's favorite pitch—he couldn't touch one.

After listening to about a 10-minute dissertation, McNally looks at Earl and says, "Earl, the only thing you know about pitching is that it was tough to hit."

❖ County Stadium

One of the great meetings Earl called came after we had lost eight of nine games. We hadn't been scoring a lot of runs and are in Milwaukee. That old stadium had a lot of history with (Hank) Aaron and Eddie Matthews. Back then, Milwaukee had seen a lot of success thanks to some really good teams.

Earl stands in the middle of the clubhouse and starts letting us have it.

"First of all," he says, "you guys don't want to win badly enough. We're not getting runners in from third base with less than two outs. I never—ever—failed to get a runner in from third base with less than two outs. Whether it was a bunt, a sacrifice fly or I hit the ball the other way, somehow I figured out how to get the guy in (from third)."

McNally calls out from way in the back, "Yeh, but you never played higher than AA ball."

Earl doesn't bat an eye. He continues without hesitation. "The other thing is, when you're on the road, the game isn't over—I don't care how many runs you're down—until you

make the last out. And that's another thing—along with always getting the guy in from third base—I refused to make
the last out of the game."

I'm sitting there thinking, "Geez, we're here in County
Stadium in Milwaukee. I know Babe Ruth didn't play here,
but Musial played here. So did Williams, Aaron, Matthews,
and Mays. Here's our diminutive little Mickey Rooney (that
was his nickname) telling us that he never made the last out
of the game. I know that Gehrig did it (made the last out).
And I know Ruth did it. So I raise my hand.

He looks at me and says, "What do you want?"

Not "Yes, Jim," just, "What do you want?"

I say, "We all know why you never made the last out of
a game."

"Why's that?"

"They used to always pinch-hit for you."

With that Earl says, "The meeting's over. You've ruined
the mood."

❖ Yes, Earl, we're trying

We had a shortstop who won eight Gold Gloves, Mark Belanger. I'm pitching an afternoon game in Baltimore versus
the Twins. The game starts, and I walk a couple of guys.
Belanger makes two errors—which hardly ever happened.
Boog Powell, our huge MVP first baseman, loses a ball in
the sun. The Twins get two quick runs. I didn't want to give
up two runs, but the game is certainly not over. We just got
started.

Earl calls time out, walks out from the dugout, and asks
me, "Are you f*$#ing trying?"

I couldn't believe it. "Am I trying? You made out the
lineup! Why don't you ask Belanger if he's trying? Or better
yet, why don't you ask our 285-pound first baseman if he
was trying to lose that ball in the sun? What do you mean am
I f*$#ing trying?"

He shrugs. He doesn't say anything else. Just stands there.

I was ticked off. "That's all you got? You come out here and ask me if I'm trying?"

He nods. "Yeh," he says, "I want to know if you're f*$#ing trying."

"Yes, I'm trying." I look and nod toward the dugout. "Why don't you get out of here?"

That was it. He left.

That was vintage Earl. The game begins, the fielders are kicking it around, and two runs score. The one thing a pitcher does not want to hear is whether or not he's trying.

❖ Jim Palmer

Palmer tried very hard throughout his Hall of Fame career, going 268-152 in 19 seasons with the Orioles. Jim won three Cy Young Awards, won 20 games or more eight times during a nine-year span, and threw 53 shutouts—10 of them in 1975 when his ERA was a league-leading 2.09 in 323 innings of work. Jim averaged more than eight innings per start that season (25 complete games in 38 starts) and won his second Cy Young Award. A six-time All-Star, Jim also earned four Gold Gloves for fielding excellence.

Palmer was a money game pitcher, going 8-3 with a 2.61 ERA in 17 postseason appearances. At the age of 20 he threw a shutout in the World Series, defeating the Los Angeles Dodgers and Sandy Koufax 6-0 on four hits in game two to help the Orioles to a four-game sweep. Pitching for the third time in eight days, this was the final appearance of Sandy Koufax's brief but legendary career.

58

Mike Krukow

The Legend of
Sheridan's Horse

I want to say the year was 1984. I was with the Giants, and whenever we were in Chicago to play the Cubs, we always stayed downtown. The route our bus driver used through the city on the way to Wrigley Field took us by General Sheridan's Triangle at Belmont Road and Sheridan Avenue. The triangle centerpiece is a huge statue of General Sheridan riding his horse, a stallion. This horse has a set of nuts the size of a man's head—maybe even bigger.

Every time a baseball team would drive by the statue, one of the players would call out, "Don't look at the balls, it's bad luck!" It was kind of a universal ritual honored throughout the league.

This year we had a bunch of rookies on the team. Two in particular, outfielder Rob Deer and pitcher Jeff Robinson, were on the team bus. One day we're just messing around on the bus ride over, so I stand up and start doing my Jimmy Swaggert imitation, addressing the boys with passion and emotion.

"There's no heart in these rookies anymore," I tell them. "Rookies used to come up (to the Big Leagues) and paint the balls on the horse the team colors. The Dodgers painted them blue. If you were on the Giants, you painted them orange. If you were with the Pirates, those balls were painted yellow.

"We have a bunch of slapdick kids now—a bunch of 'I' guys. None who really gets the concept of what it's like to be a Big Leaguer." I am full on, blowing some severe smoke up their asses.

The rookies listen. They take it all in. The next day is getaway day. We board the bus, leave the hotel, and drive out toward Wrigley. The bus driver takes his normal route, exiting the freeway, passing by General Sheridan's Triangle, and the horse is sporting the greatest set of orange nuts possible. It is absolutely hysterical. Those two rookies, Rob Deer and Jeff Robinson, were the first two guys to paint the horse's balls.

From there the legend began to grow. The next year, 1985, our team is doing real well; we have a bunch of kids like Robbie Thompson and Will Clark who can really play. We have so many rookies, they take the team bus to get the job done. KCBU, the channel that broadcast Giant games back home, asked if they can go with the guys and film it. We relent and say okay.

We stop the bus at the Triangle, the cameraman gets out and sets up, and he's followed by the exiting onslaught of players. It has rained a little bit that night, so General Sheridan and the horse are kind of slippery. It is hilarious watching nine guys climb up this thing, hanging on for dear life while trying to spray paint the wet horse balls of an old, historic statue. Their chosen color is bright fluorescent orange.

It was awesome. To this day, I can still see it. The rooks were on that statue like rats on a hunk of cheese. It was choreographed, we had a stopwatch, and we timed them. They painted the balls beautifully, hurried back, and hopped on the bus. We drove around the block, so we could circle around and take a look.

"Nope," one of the guys said, "we missed a spot. We have to do it again." We drove the bus back around, stopped, and unloaded all the rookies. They ran back over and painted the nuts again.

The filmed piece that KCBU produced was so good the station manager decided to run it. They put it on the air during the ten o'clock news. They didn't just play the piece; they pimped it for five hours leading up to it. When we returned home to San Francisco, our general manager, Al Rosen, didn't think it was very funny.

I lied to him through my teeth. "When I was a rookie with the Cubs," I said, "we got caught by the cops (doing it). They took me to the precinct house, and I had to sign my name in a book along with all the other guys through the years that got caught. I look at the names. There is Ernie Banks, there is Billy Williams. Gehrig was even on the list."

Rosen and his guys bought it: hook, line, and sinker.

Like everything else in baseball, things circle the league in about an hour and a half, and a baseball tradition is born. When several of the guys moved on to other teams, they took the legacy of Sherman's Triangle along.

The legend of the horse grew to the point that when guys went to teams, they made sure their rookies painted the horse's balls. The Chicago police department got in on it too and started setting all those guys up. The cops knew Otis, the visiting clubhouse guy (now the home clubbie), and Otis set things up where the vice detectives would come in the morning after and bust the players who did it.

The detectives would arrest the guys right there in the clubhouse, in front of everybody. It was hysterical how guys reacted when they learned they were going to jail. Some guys would turn their teammates in, some guys wouldn't. It was beautiful.

For years Sherman's Triangle was a great baseball tradition. Finally, it reached the point that the city of Chicago got tired of forking over budget money to clean the horse balls each time they were painted. It was funny at first, but one day the city decided they'd had enough. From that point forward, they would prosecute.

So ended the baseball tradition of Sheridan's horse.

❖ Olson's take on Sheridan's horse

In 1999, I was with the Arizona Diamondbacks. I had heard about "the painting of the balls" throughout my career, but

I came up in the American League, and American Leaguers never passed by the Triangle since Comiskey is in a different area of Chicago. Although I had been in the Majors for a decade, I had never seen the statue nor its painted testicles.

At one point in 1999, we had seven or eight rookies up on the big club and found ourselves in Chicago. We decided we'd paint the statue after our day game against the Cubs and scheduled our paint party for post-game. We secured the paint early in the morning, and the hit was on. At 10:00 p.m. we piled all eight or nine of us into two cabs and rode to the Triangle.

I kept both cabs waiting at the curb as the rookies spilled out, ran over, and spray painted the horse's nuts, raced back, and piled back inside the taxis. They were like the Marx brothers. We made a clean getaway.

The best part of the gag happens the next day. Our team bus arrives at the ballpark, and within 15 minutes, two vice cops show up. This isn't a couple guys playing good cop/bad cop—this is two guys playing bad cop/worse cop. I don't know how or why they choose to single out Erubial Durazo, but "Ruby" is fingered as the culprit.

When the cops enter the clubhouse, they go straight to his locker. I am cowering in the food room, watching and listening. The officers are yelling at Ruby and reading him the riot act. After a few minutes, they start squeezing him to find out who else was involved.

Ruby pretends not to understand. He replies in Spanish, "No habla." Since Durazo won't turn anyone else in, the police order him to change back into his street clothes. They stand nearby as he changes. As soon as he's dressed, they slap on a pair of handcuffs. As the cops ready to lead Ruby out of the clubhouse, they give him one final chance to reveal who else participated.

"No habla," he repeats. "No habla."

As Ruby is escorted to the clubhouse, I look around to the other rookies involved. Only one, pitcher Erik Sabel, isn't watching Durazo's dramatic exit. Erik has just come

The Legend of Sheridan's Horse

up within the past few weeks and refuses to watch. He is sitting on his chair in front of his locker, his face buried in his hands. From the side I can see a portion of his face. He is whiter than a sheet of paper.

❖ Mike Krukow

Mike Krukow, fondly known as "The Polish Prince," pitched 14 seasons in the National League and won 124 games. In 1986, the tall right-hander went 20-9 and was named to the All-Star team. Mike completed 10 of 32 starts that season with two shutouts. He threw 245 innings with a 3.05 ERA to finish third in voting for the Cy Young Award behind Mike Scott and Fernando Valenzuela.

A good hitting pitcher, Mike hit five home runs during his career. He pitched his final seven seasons for the San Francisco Giants and remained in the Bay Area after retiring in 1989. A staunch defender of Barry Bonds throughout the controversial end of Barry's career, Krukow is a popular Bay Area broadcaster on Giants baseball telecasts.

❖ The Sheridan Triangle statue

Famed sculptor Gutzon Borglum, the same man who sculpted the presidents' likenesses from the granite of Mt. Rushmore, sculpted Chicago's legendary baseball landmark equestrian statue of General Sheridan atop his horse. The statue is located on an island at the intersection of Belmont Avenue and Sheridan Road, five minutes southeast of Wrigley Field.

Philip Henry Sheridan was a career Army officer and Union general during the Civil War. He was a close friend of Ulysses S. Grant and used scorched earth tactics to defeat Confederate forces in the Shenandoah Valley. In 1865, Sheridan's cavalry aggressively pursued Confederate General Robert E. Lee and helped force Lee's surrender at Appomattox.

After the war, Sheridan was ruthlessly cruel fighting Indians across the Great Plains. Later in life, he was instrumental in the protection and development of Yellowstone National Park. Shortly before Sheridan died, President Grover Cleveland named him a four-star general.

Nothing happened to Erubial Durazo after being led from the clubhouse in handcuffs. He was uncuffed, released, and sent back to dress for the game. Ruby's teammates applauded his willingness to take one for the team and not give anyone up—especially Erik Sabel.

59

Umpire Ed Montague

Pull Don't Push & Don't Lose the Slim-Fast

❖ Pull Don't Push

When Bobby Cox was first managing the Braves, his first go-round, we were at the San Francisco Giants' Candlestick Park—lovely, cold Candlestick Park. Bobby and I got into a big blowout. I think I called a balk on Phil Niekro. Bobby didn't like it and came out of the dugout to argue. I was umping first base, so Bobby ran out to meet me by the bag.

It didn't take long to get into a shouting match. Choice words filled the air as we stood there screaming at each other.

I tossed Bobby out of the ballgame. Bobby being Bobby, he got really animated. He stayed there at first base for quite awhile, arguing with me nose to nose.

Finally, the argument ended. Since Bobby was ejected and had to leave the field, he now had to walk all the way back to the visitor's dugout to give Jimy Williams, or whoever was going to run the club, the (lineup) cards and notes.

In Candlestick, the visitors' dugout had no direct exit leading to the clubhouse. The only way to get there was to walk all the way down the right field line before eventually veering off into the clubhouse tunnel.

Having done that, Bobby still had to leave the field and go to the clubhouse. In order to do that, he had to pass by me at first base. On the way past, he decided to once again let me know how he felt.

He's giving it to me again, and I'm going right back at him. When he finally stalks away and marches down the foul line, he stops at the big entry doors that lead to both clubhouses.

He turns back toward me and yells, "I'll kick your ass!"

I yell back, "You know where the parking lot is!"

Now he's really pissed off.

Bobby pivots away and charges forward into the big double-doors and angrily shoves them open. Unfortunately for him, they don't give. Bobby bounces into them and bounces back off, losing his balance and stumbling backward—almost to the right field foul line.

Hurling another verbal knife, I yell, "Next time, try pulling!"

Bobby's furious. He storms back to the big double-doors and pulls them open. He disappears inside, and the doors close bang behind him.

The next year, Bobby leaves the Atlanta Braves and goes to Toronto to manage the Blue Jays. A few years later, he left Toronto and returned to Atlanta to again manage the Braves. I forget how many years he was gone, but one night we end up back together again at Candlestick.

That night I'm on the umpiring crew with Bob Davidson, and Bob (Davidson) gets into a shouting match with the Braves' third base coach Jimy Williams. Bob kind of threw the bait out, Jimy took it, and Bob tossed him.

Out comes Bobby (Cox). Within seconds, he's nose to nose with Davidson. Cox calls Davidson every name in the book and invents a few more.

I intervene to play good cop, bad cop. I get between the two of them and try to steer Cox away. Bobby is strong as a bull and hard to move.

I keep trying. "C'mon Bobby, let's go, let's go."

He's shouting at Davidson, and Davidson keeps shouting back. I finally look at Davidson and say, "Bob, just shut up! I'm trying to get him away."

Davidson pipes down, and finally I get Cox to start walking down the first base line. As he walks, he keeps looking back at Davidson. I'm walking alongside.

"Let's go, Bobby," I urge, "let's go. You alright?"

"Yeah, yeah, I'm alright."

Since Davidson tossed him and Bobby has to leave the field, I nod toward the right field corner and send him on his way.

"Hey, Bobby," I say, "when you get down to those two big green doors, remember they pull out."

"Awww! You remember that?!"

"How could I ever forget?"

He exited, and the game resumed.

Sometimes you have to have a little fun.

* * *

❖ Don't Lose the Slim-Fast

When Tommy Lasorda was managing the Dodgers and doing the Slim-Fast weight loss endorsement stuff, he also managed to hook up longtime veteran umpire Bruce Froemming with the company too. Bruce was doing something for Slim-Fast where they actually paid him. I'm not sure what he was doing or how things worked, but I do know Bruce was making some money.

I'm doing a game with the Dodgers, and several of us are chatting around home plate. I remember I'm working with Harry Wendlestedt and Gary Darling. They're there too. For fun, I start busting Tommy's balls.

"You give Bruce all that stuff, why don't you send us a bar or a can of something?"

Tommy being Tommy, he says, "Sure, I'll send you something after the ballgame."

I'm working first base, and Darling's got the plate. Mike Sciosia is catching for the Dodgers. Something happens, and there is a big mess at home plate. Everybody starts yelling, tempers burn, and all holy heck breaks loose.

Sciosia gets tossed. Tommy and Darling are going nose to nose. Harry, the crew chief, gets in the middle of it. Soon he's nose to nose with Tommy.

I kind of stroll down from first base and tap Harry on the shoulder. When Harry gets mad, he turns beet red. And he was redder than a stop sign.

I keep tapping his shoulder. Still arguing with Lasorda, he ignores me.

"Harry. Harry." He turns to me, sees me, but ignores me. He goes back to yelling at Tommy.

I tap on his shoulder one more time.

"Harry?" I ask politely.

He turns around.

"What?"

"Ask Tommy if this means we don't get the Slim-Fast."

That ended the argument.

* * *

❖ Ed Montague

Ed saw it all and called it all in his long, distinguished career behind the plate and on the bases. In addition to calling four All-Star Games and six World Series—his last four as crew chief—Ed also was umpiring first base in 1985 when Pete Rose singled to break Ty Cobb's all-time hit record, and he was working second base on May 28, 2006 when Barry Bonds hit his 715th home run to pass Babe Ruth for second place on the all-time list.

When Ed retired prior to the start of the 2010 season, he had called 4,369 games, eighth most in Major League history. Ed's trademark quick flick of the right hand was a signature move known to all baseball fans. He wasted little time ringing a guy up, especially a left-handed hitter.

* * *

❖ Bobby Cox

Bobby Cox was a weak-hitting third baseman who played just 220 games in the Majors. He made $10,000 playing for the Yankees in 1968 and was out of the bigs the following year at age 28.

His lasting mark on the game began emerging nine years after he retired as a player. Despite his humble playing career, Cox grew to become one of baseball greatest managers.

A four-time manager of the year and a winner in both leagues, Cox would lead the Atlanta Braves to five National League pennants and the 1995 World Series championship. He also won 10 additional Division championships, one with Toronto and nine with Atlanta.

Cox's Braves were a divisional juggernaut from 1991 through 2005. They won the division 14 of 15 years, including 11 in a row. Thirteen of those seasons, the team won 90 games or more.

When Bobby finally retired at age 70, the man who played in 220 games had managed 4,508 more. He won 2,504 and trails only Connie Mack (3,731 wins in 53 years), John McGraw (2,763 wins in 33 years), and Tony La Russa, who won 2,728.

* * *

❖ Tommy Lasorda

He may have bled Slim-Fast some of the time, but legendary Dodger loyalist Tommy Lasorda bleeds Dodger blue all the time. The pride of Norristown, PA, Lasorda is probably baseball's most famous pitcher never to have won a game. He was 0-4 in his Major League career with a lifetime ERA of 6.48. Tommy walked 119 and hit nine more in 124 innings and averaged a wild pitch every five innings.

Offensively, Tommy wasn't much better. He was 1-for-14 as a hitter, singling in 1946.

But those who can't do sometimes make the best teachers, and Lasorda willed his love for the game from mayhem on the mound to excellence in the dugout. A lifelong Dodger, Tommy was late to the game as a manager. He was 48 when he got his first opportunity—the last four games of the 1976 season—and won the pennant his first full year.

Tommy would go on to manage 21 years, his teams winning four pennants and two World Series. In 1983 and 1988, he was named National League Manager of the Year. For his career, Lasorda was 1,599-1,439 with 13 finishes in first or second place.

Tommy's vibrant, irrepressible managerial credentials were cemented in 1997, when the Veterans Committee voted him into the Baseball Hall of Fame at Cooperstown.

❖ Slim-Fast

Slim-Fast is a weight-loss brand of dietary supplements sold by Unilever. Founded in 1977, the brand offers shakes, snacks, pre-packaged meals, and health bars for those desiring to manage their weight more effectively. Diet shakes were what made the brand popular, and Lasorda an effective pitchman.

In addition to Tommy Lasorda, other Slim-Fast spokespeople have included TV celebrities Whoopi Goldberg, Kathie Lee Gifford, and Shari Belafonte.

60

Gregg Olson

Prank Wars: the Season Finale

A good way to avoid retaliation for a prank is to pull it on the final day of the season. This was a guideline I respected my entire career.

Late in my career, I was in Los Angeles with the Dodgers, and longtime Oriole catcher Rick Dempsey was now my bullpen coach. He and I had a dueling prank fest throughout the last series of the 2000 season. We were finishing in San Diego, where the bullpens are stuck out in right field.

I messed with Demper the first night. It was just jokes, seeds in the pants, the little things. The next day he struck back with some shoelace cutting.

The final game of the year is a day game, and, as always, I arrive at the ballpark real early. I beeline straight for Demper's locker and grab his jersey off its hanger. Then I cut all the buttons off the front and superglue them back on. Applied properly, superglued buttons will pop off as soon as the victim buttons up his jersey.

Then I took the scissors and cut the tips off all of his ink markers, which Demper uses to keep an elaborate, meticulous scorecard.

I was gone when Demper came in, safely out of range. I never saw him put his jersey on, but five minutes before I was due to report to the bullpen, he is huddled in front of his locker sewing. He must have taken an hour to sew his jersey buttons back on because he shows up in the bullpen in the fourth inning, four innings later than every bullpen coach is supposed to.

Demper just watches the game. He has been defeated. He doesn't even bother keeping score.

❖ Rick Dempsey

Rick broke into the Majors at 19 and was a starting and backup catcher for the next 24 years, half of them with the Baltimore Orioles. After 1,765 Major League games, he retired at 42.

Dempsey played in three World Series and won twice—with the Orioles in 1983 against Philadelphia and five years later with the Dodgers versus the Oakland A's. Just a .233 hitter during the regular season, Rick was at his best in the postseason, hitting .308 in his 14 World Series games. He was MVP of the 1983 World Series, getting five clutch hits—four doubles and a home run—and batting .385 in the Orioles' five-game victory.

Only three catchers have played in three decades, and Dempsey is one. Carlton Fisk and Tim McCarver are the other two.

After retiring as a player, Rick coached and managed in the minor leagues and coached in the Majors with both the Dodger and Oriole organizations. The son of a vaudevillian, Dempsey now does some occasional broadcasting.